"*Pragmatics in Korean and Japanese Translation* is undoubtedly a seminal addition to works on East Asian translation, featuring examples of translations from English into Korean and Japanese, and from Korean and Japanese into English. It provides diverse, timely insights on the pragmatic difficulties encountered when translating in these language pairs. The case studies involve critically acclaimed literary texts of the twenty-first century as well as highly popular graphics texts of manga and webtoons. The analyses will surely lead to productive conversations about pragmatics in translation. I highly recommend this book to students and researchers of East Asian translation and linguistics. Not limited to specialists, its accessible language and materials such as *The Hobbit* and *Harry Potter and the Philosopher's Stone* will surely attract a wider audience as well."

Young-mee Yu Cho, Associate Professor of Korean Language and
Culture, Rutgers University

"*Pragmatics in Korean and Japanese Translation* is a fantastic addition to works on translation studies. Currently there is a growing interest in Korean and Japanese pop culture, and a thirst for understanding the meanings that end up lost in translation. Translation culture has changed dramatically over the last few decades, with more and more ordinary people getting involved in and questioning translations. This book demonstrates the dynamic nature of translation. Such topics have been heavily explored in Eurocentric areas, but this book contains fascinating and novel evidence from Japan and Korea. I strongly recommended this book not only to scholars of Asian studies but to scholars in wider translation studies as well."

Mee-Jeong Park, PhD, Associate Professor and Chair, East Asian
Languages and Literatures, University of Hawaii at Manoa

Pragmatics in Korean and Japanese Translation

This book explores how the greater amount of pragmatic information encoded in Korean and Japanese can result in pragmatic (in)visibility when translating between those languages and English. Pragmatic information must be added when translating from English to Korean or Japanese and is easily lost when translating in the other direction.

This book offers an analysis of translations in Japanese and Korean of *Harry Potter and the Philosopher's Stone* and *The Hobbit, or There and Back Again* to show how the translated versions crystallise the translators' interpretations of relationships in the way characters address one another. This book discusses fan translations of Korean and Japanese to English of various popular media, observing that the emotional meanings easily lost when translating in this direction are often deemed important enough to warrant the insertion of additional explanatory material. The book additionally discusses the role of fan translation in the construction of international online communities and a heightened communal commentary on translation. Western translation commentary has historically lacked sufficient emphasis on translation to and from East Asian languages, and these case studies help to address a problem of central importance to translation to and from languages that encode interpersonal dynamics in dramatically different ways to English.

This book will be of interest to students and researchers in translation studies, particularly in Korean and Japanese translation. The book will also appeal to students and researchers of the Korean and Japanese languages.

Jieun Kiaer is Professor of Korean Linguistics at the University of Oxford. She publishes widely on East Asian translation, with particular emphasis on Korean translation. Her publications include *The Routledge Course in Korean Translation* (2018); *Translation and Literature in East Asia: Between Visibility and Invisibility*, with Jennifer Guest and Xiaofan Amy Li (2019); *Korean Literature through the Korean Wave*, with Anna Yates-Lu (2019); and *On Translating Modern Korean Poetry*, with Anna Yates-Lu and Mattho Mandersloot (2020).

Ben Cagan read Japanese and Korean at the University of Oxford from 2008 to 2013 and discovered a passion for translation studies while working on his graduation thesis: a data-driven stylometric investigation into the distinctive language features of Murakami Haruki as a translator. After studying law at the University of Law, London, and qualifying as a financial regulation lawyer, he returned to the study of translation in 2017 with a Masters in Translation at SOAS University of London. He has been a professional translator for several years.

Routledge Studies in East Asian Translation
Series Editors: Jieun Kiaer, *University of Oxford, UK*
Amy Xiaofan Li, *University College London, UK*

Routledge Studies in East Asian Translation aims to discuss issues and challenges involved in translation between Chinese, Japanese and Korean as well as from these languages into European languages with an eye to comparing the cultures of translation within East Asia and tracking some of their complex interrelationships.

Most translation theories are built on translation between European languages, with only few exceptions. However, this Eurocentric view on language and translation can be seriously limited in explaining the translation of non-European literature and scholarship, especially when it comes to translating languages outside the Indo-European family that have radically different script forms and grammatical categories, and may also be embedded in very different writing traditions and cultures. This series considers possible paradigm shifts in translation theory, arguing that translation theory and practice need to go beyond European languages and encompass a wider range of literature and scholarship.

Missionary Translators
Translations of Christian Texts in East Asia
Jieun Kiaer, Alessandro Bianchi, Giulia Falato, Pia Jolliffe, Kazue Mino and Kyungmin Yu

Understanding Korean Film
A Cross-Cultural Perspective
Jieun Kiaer and Loli Kim

Korean Wave in World Englishes
The Linguistic Impact of Korea's Popular Culture
Brittany Khedun-Burgoine and Jieun Kiaer

Pragmatics in Korean and Japanese Translation
Jieun Kiaer and Ben Cagan

For more information about this series, please visit: https://www.routledge.com/Routledge-Studies-in-East-Asian-Translation/book-series/RSEAT

Pragmatics in Korean and Japanese Translation

Jieun Kiaer and Ben Cagan

Routledge
Taylor & Francis Group

LONDON AND NEW YORK

Cover image: Getty Images

First published 2023
by Routledge
4 Park Square, Milton Park, Abingdon, Oxon OX14 4RN

and by Routledge
605 Third Avenue, New York, NY 10158

Routledge is an imprint of the Taylor & Francis Group, an informa business

© 2023 Jieun Kiaer and Ben Cagan

The right of Jieun Kiaer and Ben Cagan to be identified as authors of this
work has been asserted in accordance with sections 77 and 78 of the Copyright,
Designs and Patents Act 1988.

British Library Cataloguing-in-Publication Data
A catalogue record for this book is available from the British Library

Library of Congress Cataloging-in-Publication Data
A catalog record has been requested for this book

ISBN: 978-1-032-10868-1 (hbk)
ISBN: 978-1-032-10867-4 (pbk)
ISBN: 978-1-003-21746-6 (ebk)

DOI: 10.4324/9781003217466

Typeset in Times New Roman
by Newgen Publishing UK

Contents

Figures

Tables

Acknowledgements

Jieun Kiaer is grateful to Derek Driggs, Loli Kim, Patrick Gwillim-Thomas, and Anna Anderson for assisting the project through data collection. Jieun is also grateful to her students who participated in the pragmatics of translation seminar.

As an immunodeficient person who worked on this book during the COVID-19 pandemic, Ben Cagan would like to thank Emily for living through shielding with him, as well as the EMA and French government for rolling out life-changing prophylactic therapies to the severely clinically vulnerable.

This work was supported by the Core University Program for Korean Studies of the Ministry of Education of the Republic of Korea and Korean Studies Promotion Service at the Academy of Korean Studies (AKS-2021-OLU-2250004).

Preface

Pragmatics matter in translation. This is particularly true for translation between East Asian languages and English, where pragmatic issues can become a major source of difficulty, both during the translation process and in dissatisfaction from readers. If we take for granted a broad understanding of translation as the creation of a text in a target language based in some way (and there is of course enormous scope for controversy on the nature of this relationship) on a source text written in another language, then we can probably take it as a corollary that a greater difference between the source and target language leads to greater complexity in the translation process.

This is not the place for a taxonomy of languages and all the ways that they can differ, but we should note that such a taxonomy is broadly possible, and that the significance of the difference between languages is far from constant. Translation to and from East Asian languages has received relatively little attention in the discourse surrounding translation in "the West." On the one hand, this is understandable: we can hardly criticise Cicero, for example, for not discussing the languages of Korea and Japan. Nevertheless, another result of the restricted contact between European and East Asian languages (which obviated the need for the discussion of associated translation problems) is that languages from Europe are in many ways far more different from languages from Asia than from other European languages, and vice versa.

Some of these differences are easy for an English speaker to understand. For example, English may tend to have a subject-verb-object ordered syntax, but it is not difficult to grasp the idea of a verb-final structure. This is a rearrangement of familiar categories. The freer (or even preferred) omission of arguments may be more difficult to account for, or even somewhat uncomfortable for English speakers. But perhaps more fundamental is the way that East Asian languages such as Korean and Japanese reflect interpersonal relations in a much more diverse and complex manner than English and other Western European languages (Kiaer 2020). It would not be going too far to say that one cannot confidently form an utterance in Korean or Japanese without an idea of who is speaking and to whom. Nobel

Prize-winning theoretical physicist Richard Feynman (1985/2022: 245–6), for example, told an anecdote about refusing to accept the need to use different predicate forms in Japanese to reflect levels of politeness, and giving up his study of the language as a result. If this kind of difference is a deal-breaker for a mind as capable as Mr Feynman's, we daresay there are some others who would experience similar difficulties, and that this is an issue that deserves some attention.

The fact that pragmatic factors are overtly encoded for to a greater level in Korean and Japanese than in English leads to meanings related to issues such as politeness and intimacy being easily lost (or, indeed, added) in translation. In the past, translation between these regions has predominantly occurred from English into the East Asian languages. The body of literature translated from East Asian languages into English is constantly growing, however, so there is real demand to capture these pragmatic meanings in a culturally appropriate manner. Without diving into the chicken-and-egg debate about the relationship between linguistic categories as evidence or cause of significance to speakers of a given language, Japanese and Korean speakers often deem the pragmatic information presented in those languages as important. It is therefore no surprise that, with the explosion of prestige attracted by, for instance, Korean media such as *Parasite* and *Squid Game*, that much of the criticism one sees from source language speakers concerning translations into English concerns an impression that pragmatic meanings (relating to items such as address terms) have been inadequately captured.

We have no intention of weighing in here on a prescriptive programme for translation. We do note, however, that the historical preference in the anglophone world for translations that are naturalising means that acceptability to the target readership has been prioritised over adequacy to the source text. As English does not encode pragmatic meaning to the same extent as Korean and Japanese, the translator is presented with the choice of trying to compensate with strategies that may be unwieldy and unnatural to target-language readers, or to allow the loss of some of these meanings. Increasing globalisation and connectivity through social media mean that critical voices from source-language speakers are becoming more visible than ever before, and so these pragmatic differences have recently attracted some attention in the media.

Translation in the other direction, from English to East Asian languages such as Korean and Japanese, is no less interesting. Here, the translator's interpretation of the pragmatic contexts of the source text have to be crystallised and made overt if the target text is to come across as natural. The greater prestige that European language source texts have had in these cultures may mean that the drive for naturalisation is not as extreme in these areas, but translators are a long way from flattening out the target-language structures tied to pragmatic meaning.

We have already noted that we have no intention of telling translators what to do. Instead, we thought it might be interesting, and helpful, to present some case studies of translation between these languages in order to highlight the nature and complexity of some of these problems, as well as how translators have treated them in some cases. Our hope is that this can serve as inspiration, or a starting point, for further investigation into this vast and neglected area.

Preliminaries

Romanisation conventions

At least twenty different systems for the romanisation of Korean have appeared in printed media, of which the McCune-Reischauer, Yale, and Revised Romanisation systems are the most widely accepted. In this text, apart from when presenting direct quotations from sources that use another form of romanisation, it is the Revised Romanisation system that has been adopted. Korean *hangeul* script is provided (at least with the first occurrence) alongside romanisations of Korean words.

For Japanese, we have adopted the revised Hepburn system of Japanese, with the same exception of extracts of quoted material where the source uses another system. Another exception has been the romanisation of words that have themselves been transliterated into Japanese in the first place. For example, the word "hobbit" is written in Japanese as ホビット, which would strictly be rendered back as *hobitto* under the revised Hepburn system but has instead been romanised as *hobbit*.

For both Korean and Japanese, quotations from the translations into those languages of *Harry Potter and the Philosopher's Stone* and *The Hobbit, or There and Back Again* are provided in the orthography as they appear in those translations when presented for comparison alongside the source texts.

References

Some translated texts are treated in this book. In the Bibliography, these are identified by the name of the translator, although we identify the source text within such citations.

1 Pragmatic (In)Visibility

This chapter discusses translational invisibility and introduces the notion of "pragmatic (in)visibility," as well as addressing the growing demand to produce balanced and culturally appropriate translations between East Asian languages and English. Although this demand itself is not new, it is becoming more and more acutely felt as East Asian popular culture and literature grow in international popularity. New attention to the subject has particularly been generated by the global popularity of South Korean popular culture, most notably by the television show *Squid Game* (2021), which received four nominations and one win at the Golden Globe Awards (Seo and Owoseje 2022), on the tail of Bong Joon-ho's feature film *Parasite* (2019), which won four Academy Awards, a Golden Globe Award, and two BAFTA Awards, among many others.

1.1 Rethinking Translation

In the past century, Asian languages have been severely under-represented in anglophone translation. On the one hand, with English being the long-standing lingua franca, one can see how Asian texts may become less of a priority. On the other hand, the significant differences found in the linguistic and cultural repertoires of Asian and European languages make it difficult to understand how particular practical issues concerning fidelity in translation to and from these languages, and likewise frameworks in research that take a view of these cultural contexts' subjects, haven't received more attention. If anything, the linguistic disparity indicates a need for more, as opposed to less, effort in more adequately representing Asian texts. Comprehension of foreign texts, as they were intended to be read in their source languages, relies upon contextualisation within their respective cultures and histories. It is only through this that the magnitude of the cultural discourses the texts contain can be engaged with, and the culturally accrued modes of making sense needed to understand faithful translations are learnt. Translations of Asian texts, however, have traditionally undergone the whitewashing of so-called "naturalisation," a strategy that tends towards the creation of a text suiting

DOI: 10.4324/9781003217466-1

the palette of target audiences – typically Westernisation or Anglicisation (Kiaer 2017).

A simple example of whitewashing Asian texts can be seen in the Eurocentric tradition of calling characters by their first names in literary fiction. East Asians, for instance, rarely call each other by name, with names never used except for between childhood friends of equal age and social status or rank in regions like Korea. Using names in the target text in locations where they aren't used in a source text – and where they wouldn't normally be used in the source language – is disruptive with respect to source-language structures; but this is far from the full extent of the problem. In East Asia, the use of address terms expresses much more than one's identity or one's relationship with the addressee. Layers of interpersonal and attitudinal meanings are often constructed through the link between a given address term and other multifarious, sometimes multimodal, elements – from the social status of interlocuters, their relationship, and developments within that relationship, to their likes and dislikes, emotions, evaluation of one another, and even whether the speaker is taking an antagonistic or sarcastic position. Even with the simple example of replacing an address term with a name, there is an immediate and considerable loss of meaning from source text to target text – to put this in other words, the complex fabric of interwoven pragmatic meaning is rendered invisible.

The readability of translated Asian texts has been prioritised over faithfulness to such meanings, with reformulations for the purpose of "helping" the target audience, of putting the text into familiar patterns to ease comprehension. This debate was perhaps most clearly set out in Schleiermacher's (1813/2021: 56) famous maxim: "Either the translator leaves the writer in peace as much as possible and moves the reader toward him, or he leaves the reader in peace as much as possible and moves the writer toward him." In more common parlance, this is the same question of how "literal" or "free" a translation should be (or is, depending on whether the analysis is prescriptive or descriptive), which, as noted by Steiner (1998), has been ubiquitous throughout the history of translation theory: from Cicero and St. Jerome, through Dryden and Schleiermacher, right up to the twentieth century.[1] Venuti (2019: 1) also argued that this fixation reflects an instrumentalist approach to translation, predicated on the idea that translation is "the reproduction or transfer of an invariant that is contained in or caused by the source text, an invariant form, meaning, or effect." Regardless of whether one views this "literal" versus "free" continuum in those terms (or according to the terminology seemingly recreated for any new iteration of such an approach, e.g., Dryden's (1680/2021) metaphrase and paraphrase, Nida's (1964) formal equivalence versus dynamic equivalence, Newmark's (1981) semantic translation versus communicative translation, Toury's (1995/2012) separation of norms requiring translation adequacy versus translation acceptability, etc.), or if one eschews this framework altogether in favour of a hermeneutic approach to translation, recognising the complexity of meaning and interpretation already present in the source text as well as in the translation process, the idea remains that a translator has to make choices about what meanings to attempt to convey in the target text, and how to do so.

Venuti (1995/2017) has described how naturalisation is overwhelmingly the standard practice for contemporary literary translation in British and American cultures, whereby a translation is judged as acceptable when it reads fluently and appears transparent, hiding the phenomenon of translation and making it appear as if there is complete transparency in translation, that the English-language reader has full access to the meaning(s) in the original text (taking for granted that such meaning(s) is/are fixed). Venuti argues that the "translator's invisibility is symptomatic of a complacency in British and American relations with cultural others, a complacency that can be described-without too much exaggeration-as imperialistic abroad and xenophobic at home" (13). Venuti himself proposed shattering the illusion of fully transparent translation through a foreignising approach, whereby "the ethnocentric violence that every act of translating wreaks on a foreign text is matched by a violent disruption of receiving cultural values that challenges forms of domination" (121).

This extreme tendency to naturalisation in translation is also a missed opportunity based on a circular argument: the very gap in cultural understanding responsible for the apparent requirement to naturalise texts is also used as grounds to avoid filling that gap. The proposition that this is a missed opportunity is not merely speculation. The growing demand to reduce conventional levels of naturalisation is being demonstrated before our very eyes as Korean film and television fans express a desire to understand what is *really* happening beyond the information presented to them in the subtitles. Similarly, interest in understanding what is really in Korean texts has so far culminated in twenty-six Korean words even making their way into the *Oxford English Dictionary*. Moreover, this is by no means an issue isolated solely to translation, but one which infiltrates Asian textual research on a broader scale. Researchers have also traditionally favoured Eurocentric frameworks for the interpretation of texts, and there is a general lack of cross-cultural perspectives able to recognise the severity of the limitations faced because of untranslatability (Matron 2010). Just as there have been calls for greater visibility in subtitles, so too are researchers now calling for more cross-cultural frameworks (Kiaer and Kim 2021a; Kiaer and Kim 2021b., Kim and Kiaer 2021).

Thus, until now there has been an imbalance, propagating linguistic and cultural "invisibility" (Kiaer 2019) and excluding Asian languages and cultures by preventing engagement with the meanings in their texts. However, this is beginning to change. East Asian texts in particular are beginning to gain visibility. In literary translation, for instance, we increasingly see the retention of cultural elements from the original language embedded within the English target text. One prominent example is the English translation of Han Kang's much celebrated novel *The Vegetarian* (2007), translated into English by Deborah Smith. The translation was rendered so that specific cultural expressions were made invisible, in order for the novel to be received without resistance by anglophone European readers, but the pragmatic system embedded in the Korean language was made visible in some respects for the sake of narrative clarity. One such strategy was the retention of Korean address terms through more literal translation into English, rather than their replacement with names. For example, *cheohyeong* (처형; "wife's older sister/sister-in-law") is translated as "sister-in-law," and *cheonam* (처남; "wife's brother/brother-in-law") is translated as "brother-in-law." Addressing someone as "sister-in-law" rather than their name may feel unnatural in English but, in this case, the use of characters' names would have meant the loss of vital pragmatic meanings – primarily the value and role that the characters hold within the family. Reverence and filial piety are significant in Korean households and so preserving address terms in the translation can be seen as a structural manifestation of this system within the narrative, making the rigidity of the hierarchical system in the social and cultural landscape and how centrally it functions within a familial setting tangible for readers (e.g., the children having to call the protagonist's father-in-law "Father" rather than "Dad"). This then extends to understanding of characters' attitudes, emotions, and personalities, such as the sister-in-law's dedication and the brother-in-law's disinterest.

Another recent example of visibility being brought to an English translation of a Korean literary text is Cho Nam-joo's *Kim Ji-young: Born 1982* (2016), which was translated into English by Jamie Chang. In the English translation, when the main character Ji-young assumes the identity of her own mother when speaking to her husband, she addresses him as "Jung *seoba-ahng*," which is a direct alliteration of the Korean word *seobang* (서방), and one that maintains the extended sound effect of lamentation of *seobang* to *seoba-ahng* (서바앙) as is presented in the original. Without some form of recognition of the way that interpersonal relations between Ji-young and her family members are reflected in the Korean when she assumes the identity of her mother during her episodes of mental unwellness, a great deal of compensatory measures would most likely have been needed to prevent a loss of coherence in the English. These pragmatic expressions, invisible when simply anglicised in translation, are vital for making sense of what is happening.

Literary translation into English from Japanese has similarly seen some attempts to capture the more complex approach to terms of address in the source language. Edwin McClellan's (1968/2010) translation of Natsume Sōseki's (1914) *Kokoro* (こころ) adopts the term "Sensei," for example. More explicit references to more varied terms of address are generally restricted to where the source text itself discusses them – that is to say, translators tend to bring out something of this complexity when address terms are mentioned, rather than simply used. An example from Murakami Haruki's (2013/2015) *Colorless Tsukuru Tazaki and His Years of Pilgrimage* (色彩を持たない多崎つくると、彼の巡礼の年) and Philip Gabriel's (2014) translation of the same text follow.

十代の頃、アオとアカとつくるは「おれ・おまえ」と呼び合ってい
た。しかし十六年ぶりに顔を合わせたときそんな親しい呼び方が「持
ちに馴染まなくなっていることにつくるは気づいた。彼は相変わら
ずつくるを「おまえ」と呼び、自分を「おれ」と呼んでいたが、つ
くるにはそれがすんなりとできなかった。そういうくだけた呼び方
は、彼にとってもう自然なことではなくなっていた。

(Murakami 2013/2015: 210)

Back when they were teenagers, Ao, Aka, and Tsukuru had used the
rough, masculine pronouns *ore* and *omae* – "I" and "you" – when they
talked to each other, but Tsukuru realized now, seeing them sixteen years
later, that this form of address no longer felt right. Ao and Aka still
called him *omae*, and referred to themselves as *ore*, but this casual way of
speaking no longer came so easily to Tsukuru.

(Gabriel 2014: 148)

自分が相手に向かって「おまえ」と呼びかけていたことに、つくる
はふと気づいた。それは最後になって自然に口から出てきた。

(Murakami 2013/2015: 235–6)

Tsukuru suddenly realized he was using the familiar *omae* to address
Aka. It came out naturally at the end.

(Gabriel 2014: 166)

The relationship of the protagonist to the group of friends from his youth, who
he understands to have ostracised him for unknown reasons, is a central theme
of the book. One wonders whether, had Murakami not himself mentioned
these pronouns rather than simply use them, the translator would have been
motivated (or felt able, within the wider context of industry pressures towards
naturalisation) to convey the important pragmatic meanings involved in their
use to the English-language reader. It is still not clear to the English-language
reader what alternative pronouns the protagonist feels more comfortable
using, nor at what point he shifted to *omae* in the conversation. The translator
(or rather, the nexus of people involved in source-text production, including
of course Gabriel but also any and all editors and other individuals who may
have been involved in such decisions) would appear to have decided that these
meanings are not sufficiently important to override the general naturalising
norms of translation into the anglophone world.

Most significantly perhaps, as touched on earlier, visibility has been
brought to the forefront in film and television. One of the watershed moments
for the public raising issues of invisibility was following the release of *Parasite*
(2019). In one of the numerous online articles by bilinguals that followed
the film's release, Cho (2020) explains her experience as a bilingual Korean
American, stating that she immediately noticed "the peculiarity of translating
Korean into English text," followed by her realisation that "[t]he subtitles are

not for me… they're for American audiences." In fact, Bong Joon-ho himself, whether intentionally or not, drew attention to invisibility at the Academy awards during his acceptance speech for Best Picture, when he referred to subtitles as "the one-inch-tall barrier." Then, most recently, amid the media storm surrounding *Squid Game*, Korean American Young-mi Mayer posted on TikTok detailing the severe invisibility she observed while watching the series as a bilingual. Her post went viral, drawing the attention of mainstream media outlets. In her TikTok post, Young-mi stated, "I just watched *Squid Game* and I am fluent in Korean and I had the English subtitles on and noticed that you're missing so much from the English subtitles." She also took to Twitter to tweet, "I'm fluent in Korean and I watched *Squid Game* with English subtitles and if you don't understand Korean you didn't really watch the same show. Translation was so bad. The dialogue was written so well and zero of it was preserved."

Underpinning the interest of the public in invisibility is the Korean Wave that, in the current era of online entertainment and social-media-led communication, has reached a new peak in global popularity. This new phase of development is marked by Korean popular culture entering the mainstream, and the facilitation of East Asian high cultures' transference into the Western social sphere. The Korean Wave has seen the emergence of fans with a notably high interest in semiotic production and participation. The crest of this wave, and fans' diligence in utilising forms of "high culture" (e.g., Korean language or non-verbal gestures) as a means of participation, has been like a trojan horse: details that would normally be overlooked by consumers of popular culture movements have been transported within popular culture into the mainstream.

The shift from low-to-high culture is visible in the formal recognition of Korean words within the English language, as noted earlier, but it can also be observed in the increase of publications that promote Korean and other East Asian ideological concepts in the West as a means of improving one's life. Euny Hong's *The Power of Nunchi: The Korean Secret to Happiness and Success* (2019), which promotes the Korean cultural concept of *nunchi* (emotional intelligence) as a means of improving one's life, is one of the most recent.

1.2 Defining Pragmatic Invisibility

The concept of "(in)visibility," not to be confused with Venuti's "translator's invisibility" (1995, 2008, 2018; discussed earlier), was first referred to from a phenomenological perspective with Scott's (2012: 62) suggestion that the invisibility of elements in the original text is a "latent multi-perspectivalism" that translators and readers of translated texts "can never properly achieve." This description indicates that a certain level of invisibility is inevitable, and also that there is far more to investigate in Asian texts than may be reflected in their English translations. The terms "(in)visibility/(in)visibles" were then coined by Kiaer (2019) to refer to the plus and minus value of linguistic forms and functions that do not exist in either the source texts (ST) and languages (SL) or in the target languages (TL) in Korean–English translations, and so cannot be translated. This is a notion that has long been in need of attention, spanning broadly across fields of research that deal with texts, including (but not limited to): linguistics (see Kiaer 2017, Kiaer 2019), translation (see House 2002) film (see Willemen 2006, Higson 2000), culture (see Bhabha 1994), Asian gesture (see Kiaer and Kim, forthcoming), and semiotics, and even recently in online visual communication.

Among all the forms of invisibility, pragmatic (or "socio-pragmatic") invisibility is one of the biggest hurdles, and, along with cultural elements, is potentially the most prolific form of invisibility encountered in the translation of Asian texts. The term "pragmatic invisibility" refers to the meanings in a language that become invisible when the pragmatic nature of a language can't be accurately translated into another, due to the differences between the languages in question (Kiaer 2019). Pragmatic "invisibles" are most prevalent in translation between languages that do not share some cultural consensus. Translation between French and Spanish, for example, results in less pragmatic invisibility because of their greater proximity and broader cultural similarity. English, on the other hand, has less of a cultural overlap with Asian languages, and so translation of an Asian text into English results in more significant pragmatic invisibility (Kiaer, Guest & Li 2019; Kiaer 2020b).

In Asian languages, social pragmatics have far greater diversity and complexity than in European languages; this is especially true of East Asian languages like Korean (Kiaer 2017). Similarly, Hasegawa (2012: 56–7) borrows Peirce's concept of "indexical meaning"[2] to argue that Japanese "customarily encodes 'too much' indexical meaning" by comparison to English. The interpersonal dynamics are complex and generate multi-layered meanings, with linguistic and non-verbal expressions that express hierarchy, intimacy, distance, and (in)formality, and through which attitudes and emotions are conveyed, motivations and intentions implied, and personalities characterised (Kiaer and Kim 2021a). This socio-pragmatic richness is not found to the same degree in European languages. Although there are ways of emphasising politeness or formality in English, there are not fixed rules for doing so based on the relation between speaker and hearer. For example, an English-speaker might say, "Excuse me, sorry to bother you, but do you happen to know where the bathroom is?" if they are in a formal environment or when speaking to a stranger. In an informal situation, or when speaking to a friend, this would feel a little distant and is likely to be replaced with an equivalent such as, "Do you know where the bathroom is?"

Even though there is clearly more of an effort made in the first sentence, reflected in a more circumlocutory form, more rigidly encoded structures, such as the particles required in some languages to indicate politeness, are absent. Nor are particular address terms needed. In British English, unless using professional titles or addressing a person of nobility (e.g., sir, lord, royal highness, dame, etc.), the only other address terms that come into everyday English tend to be those used between family members. There is a variety of address terms that can be used between family members, though selecting one is not enforced by hierarchy (in Korean, a daughter-in-law uses the more respectful *abeonim* to address her father-in-law, while she may call her father the informal *abba*). Of the variations available for addressing a single person, the choice is more usually made on an individual basis in British English. For example, a British child may refer to their mother as "mother," "mummy," "mum," "mamma," and "mama," with "mum" or "mummy" being used most frequently in the UK, and "mummy" often preferred by children rather than adults. Likewise, there is "father," "daddy," "dad," "papa," and "pa," with "dad" or "daddy" being used most frequently, and "daddy" being used more by children. There are also variations such as aunty, auntie, or aunt. A person might also generally call their mother "mum," and only use the word "mother" (which has a more formal feel) to exaggerate their love for their mother, or for humorous or dramatic effect. Likewise, because the use of "mummy" is more common among younger children, the use of this term by adults can be motivated by a desire to achieve a humorous or cute effect. Norms may vary for each family in terms of to how these terms are used and how they can be more creatively manipulated.

Both the inventory and amount of creative licence with which a speaker uses terms of address in English differ from East Asian languages. Speakers of English have a choice often lacking in Asian languages. For example, the latter of our examples, "Do you know where the bathroom is?," which could be used appropriately in an informal interaction, could also be used when speaking to a stranger or in a formal situation without risking serious offense. Indeed, strategies for politeness in British English, tend to involve "making an effort to be nice" by "impositioning oneself" whether this be through verbal language, non-verbal gestures, or the actions that are being undertaken. Examples include opening the door for someone, letting someone go in front in a queue, or asking someone, "Would you mind if..." or "Would it be okay if... (e.g., I use the bathroom/take one of these/do it in a moment)." In Asian languages such as Korean, Thai, Japanese, and Chinese, however, one's place is clearly defined, and interpretation of one's pragmatic expressions is thus far more limited as a result.

Table 1.1 provides a selection of examples of the "meaning potentials" that can commonly arise through the use of pragmatic expressions, in a range of social dynamics, and why pragmatic invisibility often occurs in relation to such cases. Representative examples of Korean–English pragmatic invisibility will be presented on this occasion, due to their vast differences and subsequent ability to illustrate it well (Kiaer 2017).

Table 1.1 Examples of invisibility between Koreans and Anglophone Europeans

Korean pragmatic expression	Verbal (V)/non-verbal (NV)	Social dynamic (speaker–hearer/ gesturer–receiver)	Common meaning potentials	Invisibility for Europeans
Patting	NV	Senior–Junior	Care/Encouragement/ Comfort	/
		Junior–Senior	Belittlement/ Antagonising/ Sarcasm/Self-importance/ Inconsideration/ Close relationship/ Overstepping boundaries	Rank does not affect patting as a rule, so its meaning can be positive or negative. How it is interpreted depends on the condition of the relationship of the individuals and context of the interaction.
Touch (skinship)	NV	Senior–Junior	Care/Encouragement/ Comfort	/
		Junior–Senior	Belittlement/ Antagonising/ Self-importance/ Inconsideration/ Overstepping boundaries	Rank does not affect touch as a rule…
		Equals/ Intimate relationship regardless of hierarchy	Close relationship/ Developing relationship	Not always a signifier of intimacy or growing intimacy by anyone.
One-handed giving/ receiving	NV	Senior–Junior	Gesturer is senior.	Has no meaning.
		Junior–Senior	Aggression/ Confrontation	Has no meaning.
		Equals/ Intimate relationship regardless of hierarchy	Gesturer is an equal and interlocutors have known each other for a long time.	Has no meaning.

(continued)

Table 1.1 Cont.

Korean pragmatic expression	Verbal (V)/non-verbal (NV)	Social dynamic (speaker–hearer/gesturer–receiver)	Common meaning potentials	Invisibility for Europeans
Two-handed giving/receiving	NV	Senior–Junior	Gesturer is scared/Junior possesses something desired or valued by the gesturer/The situation is unorthodox.	Has no meaning.
		Junior–Senior	Gesturer is junior/Gesturer values senior.	Has no meaning.
Hapsyoche (합쇼체) speech style (formal polite)	V	Senior–Junior	Speaker is scared/Junior possesses something desired or valued by the gesturer/The situation is unorthodox/The situation is formal.	Has no meaning.
		Junior–Senior	Speaker is junior/Speaker values senior/The situation is formal.	Has no meaning.
Haeyoche (합쇼체) speech style (informal polite)	V	Senior–Junior	Speaker is scared/Junior possesses something desired or valued by the speaker/The situation is unorthodox.	Has no meaning.
		Junior–Senior	Speaker is junior/Speaker values senior.	Has no meaning.
Haeche (해요체) speech style (informal/ "half-talk")	V	Senior–Junior	Speaker is senior.	Has no meaning.
		Junior–Senior	Confrontational/ Aggression/Speaker does not value senior.	Has no meaning.
-nim (님)	V	Senior–Junior	Speaker is scared/ The situation is unorthodox.	Has no meaning.
		Junior–Senior	Speaker is junior/Speaker values senior.	Has no meaning.
-A (아)/*-Ya* (야)	V	Senior–Junior	Speaker is senior.	Has no meaning.
		Junior–Senior	Confrontational/ Aggression/Speaker does not value senior.	Has no meaning.

Note: In the "Invisibility for Europeans" column, "/" indicates potential visibility. For example, patting by a senior to a junior to encourage them or express care could be understood by European audiences. It is simply not understood from a hierarchical perspective but rather as one human showing care to another.

1.3 The Complication of Multimodal Modulation

To complicate matters further, interpersonal dynamics are not fixed in Asian languages, but rather in constant fluctuation. This means that in Asian languages one must be in a constant state of evaluation: How close is our relationship? Where (location) are we? Who can see or hear our interaction? Are we discussing a sensitive matter that requires tact? Speech styles, address terms, and accompanying non-verbal gestures are selected according to such an array of considerations. These must be renegotiated as the factors change. The ultimate goal of such consideration is generally to avoid conflict. Nevertheless, one can of course carefully manipulate one's adherence to the expected norms in order to deliberately bring about or escalate conflict.

Kiaer (2020a: 93) refers to this state of flux as "multimodal modulation" (the "multimodal modulation hypothesis"), stating the following:

> The core linguistic ability found in human communication is to be able to modulate or attune/orchestrate different levels/modes of information in a harmonious way, sensitive to the socio-pragmatic needs of each situation. If conflicting or inconsistent meanings are communicated, the communication will become socio-pragmatically inappropriate, insincere or unreliable, or convey humour or sarcasm.

This hypothesis proposes that honorifics are multifaceted and involve a vast range of variables. These include speech styles, address terms, and non-verbal honorifics (see, for example, Table 1.2), all of which need to be used in a consistent manner. For example, if one begins with honorific expressions, implying that the addressee is superior to the speaker, then the speaker must maintain this attitude throughout, lest they appear unnatural or even insincere. This is due to both semantic and pragmatic inconsistency, to put it simply, such a manner of communication would defy the logic fundamental to Korean interactions. This indicates again the potential impact of pragmatic invisibility and of the choices made in "pragmatic translation." An inconsistency in terms of address used in a communication, for instance, could lead to inferences of extreme significance, and such meanings are totally lost in a naturalising approach whereby all such address terms are reflected by the same name in English.

In European languages, on the other hand, while relationships can change – people can of course become closer or more distant or alter the dimensions of their relationships (e.g., going from friends to lovers or family members) – address terms generally settle and then remain unchanged. People tend to go by their first name, with shifts from titles such as Mr, Mrs, Ms, or even Dr to first names if relationships develop from a formal first meeting to a personal relationship. Using British English again as a representative example for continuity, on British television shows you might hear someone say, "Please call me Sam" or "Let's drop the formality, we know each other now, just Sam is fine," or, in the opposite direction, "It's Dr Brown, thank you" or "I'm Dr Brown to you, thank you!" when someone is behaving improperly informal.

Table 1.2 Examples of modulation of one- or two-handed giving/receiving as representative examples

Modulate from (pragmatic expression)	Modulate to (pragmatic expression)	Social dynamic	Meaning potentials	Invisibility for Europeans
One-handed giving/ receiving	Two-handed giving/ receiving	Senior– Junior	Gesturer has realised junior is important/ Gesturer has realised junior is dangerous/ Gesturer has been threatened.	Has no meaning.
One-handed giving/ receiving	Two-handed giving/ receiving	Junior– Senior	Junior has just realised their juniority/Junior has been scalded for rudeness and changed/Junior has given up confrontation.	Has no meaning.
Two-handed giving/ receiving	One-handed giving/ receiving	Junior– Senior	Junior has become angry/Junior and senior's relationship has become	Has no meaning.
Two-handed giving/ receiving	One-handed giving/ receiving	Senior– Junior	very close. Senior realises he is no longer in danger (fear removed)/Senior drops pretence/ Situation changed from formal to informal/Senior is not exaggerating his care any longer and has returned to status quo (this may be implicative of junior's feelings in certain scenarios).	Has no meaning.

The manner in which a person speaks can change, however, going from more formal on a first meeting to relaxed after developing a closer relationship. It is rarer to reverse a shift to more casual by reverting to the initial formal term of address, unless one wishes to purposefully emphasise the distance, for instance to show that one is upset or for humorous effect, to hide the closeness

Table 1.3 Representative examples of modulation of speech styles

Modulate from (pragmatic expression)	Modulate to (pragmatic expression)	Social dynamic	Meaning potentials	Invisibility for Europeans
Haeyoche (합쇼체) speech style (informal polite)	Haeche (해요체) speech style (informal/ "half-talk")	Junior– Senior	Junior has become angry/Junior is being inappropriate (potentially due to alcohol or illness or wishes to be in conflict).	Has no meaning.
Haeche (해요체) speech style (informal/ "half-talk"	Haeyoche (합쇼체) speech style (formal polite)	Senior– Junior	Senior is exaggerating his care for the junior/Senior is exaggerating the importance of the junior (perhaps sarcastically or to be humorous)/Senior has realised the junior is important/Senior is under threat by the junior.	Has no meaning.
-nim (님)	-a (아)/-ya (야)	Junior– Senior	Junior started threatening senior/Junior is not of sound mind.	Has no meaning.
-a (아)/-ya (야)	-nim (님)	Senior– Junior.	Senior is being sarcastic or humorous to the junior.	Has no meaning.

of a relationship, or simply for propriety in a particular context (for example, one might address a colleague as Dr Smith, despite usually calling her Jane, when introducing her at a seminar to students; see Table 1.3).

1.4 Deconstructing the Invisibility

In this section, we will take a closer look at the two primary factors that give rise to pragmatic invisibility: the cultural contexts within which pragmatic expressions are relevant and the social dynamics that diversify their meaning potentials.

1.4.1 Cultural Context Matters

The ideologies underpinning the cultural contexts by which pragmatic expressions are reasoned, employed, and interpreted are of paramount importance, for they are the root from which social communication grows. The Routledge Encyclopaedia of Philosophy defines "culture" as comprising "those aspects of human activity which are socially rather than genetically transmitted. Each social group is characterised by its own culture, which informs the thought and activity of its members in myriad ways, perceptible and imperceptible" (O'Hear, 1998). The connection between (in)visibility and the ideology of each Asian region is a complex matter, and beyond the scope of full description here. Nevertheless, there are ample examples of expressions that have a variety of pragmatic meaning potentials that depend upon the cultural context in which they are employed. Pragmatic invisibility that arises between Asians and Europeans can often be explained by major identifiable differences between collectivist and individualist ideologies; the patriarchy is still strong in Asia, but there has been significant movement away from such thinking in much of Western culture (that is to say, although patriarchal structures are very much still at play, it has at least become less defensible to adhere to them as aspirational). European culture has also been firmly based in Judeo-Christian ideology, in contrast to Asian culture's foundation in Confucian, Buddhist, Taoist, and Hinduist ideologies, among others.

1.4.2 Social Matters

Interpersonal relations are of central importance to pragmatic invisibility, and this is at the core of the disparity between the languages and cultures of anglophone Europeans and East Asians. Even if we consider for a moment the pragmatic disparity between the interpersonal familial systems of the ideologies just named, there are notable differences. Buddhism is not a family-centred ideology, and so does not have formal models for family or family life, nor does it base any of its teachings around a family model. The core focus of the ideology is on personal responsibility, detachment, and one's individual pursuit of enlightenment. This stands in stark contrast to Confucianism, which is rooted in hierarchical order and in which family is placed at the centre of one's life. In Confucianism, how one speaks and behaves is strictly regulated according to hierarchy, and filial piety demands that the younger follow their parent's instructions rather than their own desires, feelings, or beliefs. The underlying ideological concept, which extends beyond family, is called *Samgang Oryun* (the three bonds and five relations). The "three bonds" refers to the loyalty between ruler and subject, filial piety between father and son, and the devotion of the wife to her husband, and the "five relations" refers to the relationships between king and subject, father and son, husband and wife, sibling and fellow sibling, and elder and younger. Hinduism, on the other hand, has no doctrinal or ecclesiastical hierarchy, only the intricate hierarchy of the social system (which is inseparable from the religion), and gives each person a place within the community; a "caste system" that divides Hindus into four main categories – Brahmins, Kshatriyas, Vaishyas, and the Shudras. Indian families do, however, adhere to a patriarchal ideology, endorsing traditional gender roles, and placing family at the centre by respecting and caring for elders by following a "joint family" structure, in which three or four generations will all live under one roof (including uncles, aunts, nephews, nieces, and grandparents).

We will demonstrate the difference in pragmatic expressions (which result in invisibility) in relation to their underlying ideologies in Table 1.4. This

Table 1.4 How cultural context influences pragmatic expressions and their subsequent invisibility: representative examples of bowing across Asia

Type of bow	Region	Social dynamic (gesturer–receiver)	Common meaning potentials	Ideological influence
Bow (standing, at the waist, unspecified depth)	UK and Europe	By males between aristocracy according to positional hierarchy By males between royalty according to positional hierarchy By male commoners to royalty or aristocracy Between commoners of any gender, though especially men (as women often curtsey)	Greeting/Farewell/ Respect/Ceremony Greeting/Farewell/ Respect/Ceremony Greeting/Farewell/ Respect/Ceremony/ Honoured Curtain call	Historically, in Europe, bowing was common within royal courts, and when commoners or aristocracy/ royals interacted with aristocracy/ royals outside of royal courts. The depth of the bow was related to the difference in rank or the degree of respect or gratitude one wished to express. Remains as tradition. Hierarchy as a form of ceremony and refined etiquette. Early 1800s. Audience began calling for the actor/actress to come to the stage when they enjoyed the show.
Ojigi (standing, bending at the waist)	Japan	Everyone, compulsory.	Greetings/Introductions/ Goodbye/Gratitude/ Respect/Juniority/ Good will/ Starting business/ Congratulations/ Requesting a favour/Praying to the gods	Chinese Confucianism.

(continued)

Table 1.4 Cont.

Type of bow	Region	Social dynamic (gesturer–receiver)	Common meaning potentials	Ideological influence
30-/45-degree/ *baekkopinsa* "belly button bow" (standing, bending at the waist)	Korea	Junior–Senior Senior–Junior	Juniority/Greetings/ Goodbye/Gratitude/ Respect/Apology Senior is scared/ Junior has threatened senior/ Sarcasm/ Senior is not of sound mind	Neo-Confucianism
Wai (a subtle bow of the head and one's hands pressed together in front)	Thailand	Everyone	Greeting/I come in peace	Hinduism and Buddhism. Secular – historically a means of showing that one does not have a weapon.
Namaste/ Namaskar/ Namaskaram (a slight bow of the head)	Indian subcontinent	Everyone	Respect/Gratitude. In Sanskrit namaste literally translates as "bend or bow to you."	Hinduism and Buddhism. Can be religious or secular. Mentioned in the Rig Veda (c.1500 BCE), the central scripture of Hinduism, and one of the oldest of the four sacred Hindu texts.
Slight bow/nod	China	Junior–Senior	Formal greeting/Juniority/ Respect	Chinese Confucianism.
Slight bow/nod	Vietnam	Junior–Senior	Formal greeting/Juniority/ Respect	Chinese Confucianism.

	Country	Relationship	Meaning	Notes
15-degree bow/ nod	Korea	Junior–Senior	Rudeness/Disrespectful/ Junior does not value senior	Neo-Confucianism.
		Senior–Junior	Seniority/Greeting/ Goodbye/Gratitude Intimacy/Greeting/ Goodbye/Gratitude	
Kowtow (placing left hand on top of right hand)	China	Equals Male–Female Female–Male Female–Male Male–Female	Greeting/Deference	The divination text, *Yi Jing* "Book of Change" (also known as the *I-Ching*). Published late ninth century BC. Pre-Confucianism, pre-Taoism, pre-Buddhism, but used and respected since by Confucians and Taoists.
Kowtow (placing right hand on top of left hand)			Greeting/Rudeness	Male left, female right rule (with only exception of funerals, when hands are switched over).
			Greeting	The *Yi Jing* says, "乾道「男, 坤道「女。" 乾(Qian) and 坤 (Kun) are two of the right trigrams mentioned in the Book of Change. The former represents dry, heaven, sun/Yang, male and the latter represents earth, moon, and female.
There are various kinds for kowtow, so we will consider only the use of hands in the kowtow here.			Rude/Disrespectful	The *Kowtow* is fundamentally an expression of deference, so to employ incorrectly makes the expression dysfunctional.

time, examples explore the pragmatic expressions made specifically by the non-verbal gesture of bowing, adding diversity to our previous examples by including a variety of representative examples of bowing in the UK and Europe, India, Thailand, China, Japan, Vietnam, and Korea.

Table 1.4 gives only a glimpse into the differences in the use of a single gesture, but even so it is clear that the pragmatic meanings and ideology behind the gesture have significant differences. Furthermore, these differences are greatly influenced by the social dynamics under which the gesture is employed. This means that when these expressions are used, a great deal of invisibility can arise if one does not recognise an array of factors in addition to the gesture itself and its subtleties, all of which are pragmatic.

1.5 Translating Pragmatic Invisibility: Through the Lens of Film

In this section, we will present examples of pragmatic invisibility through the lens of film; this medium is capable of providing us with the means of vividly illustrating pragmatic expressions and the social factors that come into play when interpreting them. Examples of pragmatic invisibility encountered specifically by anglophone Europeans in Korean films will be provided, due to Korean's socio-pragmatic richness and the considerable pragmatic invisibility found in Korean–English translation (especially in Western cultural contexts).

1.5.1 Pragmatic Expressions Create Layers of Meaning

In our first example, we examine the layers of invisible pragmatic expressions between a group of interlocutors, in a scene from Lee Joon-ik's *The Throne* (2015). Set during a time when neo-Confucianism was the governing ideology in Korea and interpersonal relations were extremely restricted and relationships greatly strained, the film tells the true story of Crown Prince Sado, who was condemned to death by his father (King Yeongjo) due to his deteriorating mental health and behaviour; a problem rooted in the lack of love or care showed to Sado because of his father's dissatisfaction with his ability to follow Confucian etiquette. In the relevant scene, King Yeongjo's new, young, pregnant concubine behaves rudely towards Prince Sado's mother (King Yeongjo's previous favoured concubine) at the presentation of Sado's newborn son to the king following his birth. The events that take place in this scene mark a shift in both the king's attitude and Sado's mental health. The young concubine's expressions are vital in creating this narrative development, in that they rightly stimulate outrage among most of those present, apart from the king himself. His acceptance of her behaviour, which defies Neo-Confucian principles, shows the king's hypocrisy in his favouritism towards the concubine and ultimately his lack of love for Sado. This then provides something of an explanation for Sado's mental deterioration. Most importantly, most of the expressions that create these layers of meaning, which form important cohesive links to the main narrative strand, are pragmatic, giving us the opportunity to explore a number of pragmatic meaning potentials that remain invisible for anglophone European audiences.

The confrontation arises when Sado's mother raises the subject of issuing a decree for the queen's birthday, and the young concubine, who desires all the king's attention, becomes irritated by the request to direct the king's attention to another woman. She expresses her dislike of the situation by discouraging Sado's mother from bothering the king with these requests. The young concubine is in no position to make such a request, however, as she carries the lowest rank among the group. Though, perhaps more significant than her presumptuous statements are her non-verbal pragmatic expressions, the severity of which is invisible. These expressions not only show her to be taking advantage of the king and behaving strategically, but paint her as outrageous, reckless, and even cruel in her blatant lack of regard for Neo-Confucian morality. Figure 1.1 shows the young concubine sitting while interacting with Sado's mother; her posture broad and uneven, her head held high, and her bold gaze directed upwards. In a Confucian context it is considered rude for a junior to behave in such a way to a senior, but in a Neo-Confucian context it is extremely damaging to one's character. The fact that she is a woman, and a young woman at that, would only make the situation more intolerable. The young concubine is being insolent, and it sets off a chain of expressions that create layers of pragmatic invisibility. The first is the severity of the young concubine's insults, followed by the humiliation and discomfort caused for Sado, his mother, and wife who are present. Then, the king's unwillingness to scold the young concubine shows his hypocrisy and lack of love towards Sado, which in turn damages Sado's feelings.

Figure 1.1 Still from *The Throne* (2015), in which the young concubine has a broad and uneven posture, head held high, and she makes direct and prolonged eye contact, the opposite of how she is expected to behave

1.5.2 Persuasion and Manipulation

In this example, we examine a scene from *Parasite* (2019), a film that tells the story of the destitute Kim family, who scheme their way into the employment of the wealthy Park family with devastating consequences. In the scene, the Kim family's employer (before their employment with the Park family) disputes their wages due to the low quality of their work. Their son Ki-woo attempts to settle the dispute, using pragmatic expressions strategically tailored to be persuasive in their submissive etiquette, and which consequently characterise him as a manipulative, devious person.

Ki-woo lowers his head and body throughout the interaction with their employer (Figure 1.2). This non-verbal gesture shows Ki-woo is attempting to persuade the woman, and that he is insincere. These gestures are meant to be employed by juniors to seniors, but Ki-woo appears slightly older than their employer and he is also male, which means that he also has hierarchical seniority and perhaps does not need to go this far. His behaviour is purposeful, and not deferential – he is being persuasive and even manipulative. Pragmatically, his non-verbal gestures are akin to saying, "You are so much more powerful than me, and I respect you a lot," which, given the woman's limited or questionable seniority, is a clear exaggeration. The fact that Ki-woo adopts such behaviour while making a request to receive the pay that they are due, even though they have not done a good job, provides a situational context for the gesture, so that these pragmatic expressions can be interpreted as not only attempts at persuasion but with the added negative connotation of manipulation. In a European film, these non-verbal pragmatic expressions, however, would not hold this same pragmatic value, and would thus be subject to potential invisibility.

Figure 1.2   Ki-woo lowers his head and body when persuading his employer to pay his family their wages in *Parasite* (2019)

1.5.3 Pragmatic Expressions Show Ji-young Is Mentally Ill

In this example, we return to *Kim Ji-young: Born 1982*, but this time Kim Do-young's 2019 feature-film adaptation of that text. This is a drama that tells the story of an ordinary 30-something Korean woman juggling work with family, and the gender discrimination she faces in each phase of her life, which eventually leads to the deterioration of her mental health. We examine the same scene mentioned briefly prior, in which Ji-young believes she is her own mother during an outburst at her parents-in-law's home and interacts with others using pragmatic expressions appropriate for use by her mother (but not for Ji-young herself).

As explained earlier, this scene sets up the narrative, and the use of pragmatic expressions, such as address terms, are of extreme importance, because they are capable of expressing precisely what is happening to Ji-young. Accordingly, when the original novel was translated into English some of the address terms were retained. In the film, these address terms give explicit confirmation that Ji-young is suffering from a mental illness, whereby she temporarily acts as if she were (and believes that she is) her own mother. However, these pragmatic verbal and non-verbal expressions do not exist in the English language.

Multimodal modulation is the first pragmatic expression to pay attention to in the scene, as it signifies a significant change in Ji-young's demeanour and indicates pending doom. On the first day of her visit to her parents-in-law's home, Ji-young had used the non-verbal expressions of a junior, with her posture compact, head and eye gaze lowered, only speaking when spoken to, and making herself useful (Figure 1.3). On the second day, however, prompted by an inconsiderate comment by her mother-in-law, Ji-young adopts a broad and

Figure 1.3 Ji-young employing the eye gaze and head position of a junior in *Kim Ji-young: Born 1982* (2019)

Figure 1.4 Multimodal modulation: the direct eye gaze and head position of a senior in *Kim Ji-young: Born 1982* (2019)

uneven posture, raises her head, and makes direct and prolonged eye contact (Figure 1.4).

The meaning of Ji-young's non-verbal expressions is then clarified by her use of the address term *sabuin* (사부인) to address her mother-in-law. Like her non-verbal expressions, this verbal expression also has a pragmatic value, in that it is meant to be used by the mother of a child to the child's mother-in-law. This means that not only is Ji-young acting like a senior, but is speaking like one too, and specifically like her own mother. As with Ji-young's non-verbal expressions, the use of *sabuin* is also a contrast from her verbal expressions on the first day of the visit, when Ji-young called her mother-in-law *omonim* (어머님), so what we are observing here is a "multimodal" modulation. Similarly, when addressing both her father-in-law and mother-in-law together, Ji-young uses the term for parents to address their daughter's parents-in-law, *sadon* (사돈), which is consistent and therefore shows that she is sincere in what she is saying.

As a result of the pragmatic invisibility that arises from the pragmatic expressions in this scene, the gravity of what is happening may not be clear, and instead misunderstood as Ji-young simply being fed up with the apparent gender imbalance in her daily life. Most significantly, this can impact on comprehension of a larger section of the film's narrative, because Korean pragmatic expressions are so multi-layered and diverse in their meaning potential that they play a key role in the cohesion of the narrative as a whole. Depending on the subtitles, this important narrative element might only be revealed when Ji-young's husband explicitly explains to her that she has been suffering from a mental illness in which she believes she is her own mother for periods of time. This explanation is a considerable way into the film, and so the viewer risks being left in the dark for a long time.

1.5.4 Pragmatic Expressions Tell Us Sa-bok's Life Is in Disarray

In this example, we examine a scene in Jang Hoon's *A Taxi Driver* (2017), in which the protagonist Sa-bok is depicted through his pragmatic expressions as having lost his pride. Based on true events, *A Taxi Driver* tells the story of Kim Sa-bok – a widowed taxi driver from Seoul who is down on his luck and trying hard, but failing, to make ends meet to support his daughter. When driving German journalist Jürgen Hinzpeter to Gwangju, he unintentionally becomes involved in the events of the Gwangju Uprising (18–27 May 1980). In the scene, Sa-bok's difficult life and loss of pride are reflected in how he adopts non-verbal expressions commonly used by juniors – a lowered head and gaze, followed by what appears to be a 30-degree bow – when chastised by his landlord's wife for not paying the rent on time and for his daughter's misbehavior (Figure 1.5). These pragmatic expressions are important because they set the scene, showing that Sa-bok is a failure and has given up on himself.

1.5.5 Pragmatic Demotion to Express Anger and Disappointment

In this example, we examine a scene from Im Sang-soo's *The Housemaid* (2010). The film tells the story of Eun-yi, a young woman hired as a house-maid by a wealthy family. The husband, *Chaebol*³ businessman Mr Goh, seduces the naive employee, and impregnates her. When his wife and mother-in-law discover this, they plot to abort Eun-yi's pregnancy against her will. In the scene in question, Mr Goh has found out about this scheme, and he confronts his mother-in-law. Despite the extreme tension of the situation, Mr

Figure 1.5 Sa-bok lowers his head and gaze while speaking to his landlord's wife in *A Taxi Driver* (2017)

Figure 1.6 Mr Goh downgrades the term used to address his mother-in-law in *The Housemaid* (2010)

Goh does not shout at his mother-in-law. Western audiences may wonder why he doesn't appear or sound more furious, aside from the subtitle translation of one of his sentences as "Are you crazy?" However, he is in fact showing the severity of his feelings pragmatically in Korean, by simply downgrading the term of address he uses when speaking to her (not reflected in the English subtitles of Figure 1.6). He shifts from using *jangmonim* (장모님), which is the respectful term for a male to use towards his mother-in-law, to *ibayo* (이봐요), which is similar to "look here" or "listen," and then again to the second-person pronoun *dangsin* (당신), which (like second-person pronouns in general) is generally avoided by Koreans, and certainly not used towards one's mother-in-law.

1.6 The Future of Korean–English Translation

We are entering a new era of translation – a translingual environment and a hybrid culture. Faithfulness wasn't the main issue before in Korean–English translation, with the priority being accessibility – to the texts by readers and to the market by Korean products. Viewed from the perspective of polysystem theory, translation can be perceived as a system within the larger literary (or, indeed, filmic or audio-visual more generally) polysystem. Even-Zohar (2005: 45), one of the principal architects of this model, observed that a system can occupy a central or peripheral position in this polysystem, corresponding to the canonicity or non-canonicity of the repertoire belonging to that system (the determination of canonicity is made by the group that governs the polysystem). Even-Zohar (1978/2021: 194) also noted that translated literature normally occupies a peripheral, or secondary, position in the literary polysystem, which leads to a tendency for higher conservativism in translation approaches (i.e., adherence to target system norms). This corresponds well to the history of translation into English, where English literature has generally been understood as occupying a position of cultural superiority, and translations into the language have, for the most part, been deemed as acceptable to the extent that they read as fluent English texts.

Even-Zohar (1978/2021: 192) identified three scenarios in which translated literature is more likely to occupy a primary, or central, position within a given polysystem: when a literature is still "young" (i.e., the polysystem is yet to crystallise); when a literature is "weak" and/or peripheral within a larger group of literatures; and when there are turning points, crises, or literary vacuums in a literature (that is to say, where, for whatever reason, the existing models fall out of favour, and acceptable alternatives are not to be found in the native canon). Hermans (2020: 109) has suggested that these proposed scenarios, which would appear to require value judgments uncharacteristic of a theoretical model presented as objective, "make more sense if we take them as referring to perceptions from within the system." Although it would feel like something of a push to describe the situation with respect to the translation of East Asian literature into English as neatly fitting any of these three scenarios, there is an argument to be made that the first is of some relevance. Although we are a long way from being able to describe literature written in English as "weak," peripheral, or secondary within the anglophone literary polysystem, we are experiencing movement in the relative centrality of cultural products of East Asian origin. Accordingly, we might expect that there is room (or even an expectation) for translations from these sources into English to shift, even if only marginally, from an approach based on acceptability to the target culture to one of adequacy with respect to the source.[4]

That is to say, now that Korean (and Japanese) products have gone mainstream, it is no surprise that one is observing greater weight being given to calls to review the balance between acceptability and adequacy in the translation of texts from these sources – be they literary or filmic. This is not only for those who are already actively consuming such products but also for the wider public who increasingly come into contact with them, in order to carve out a future in which higher degrees of naturalisation are not a perceived or real necessity for accessibility.

Notes

1 Readers approaching this text from a background in East Asian linguistics rather than Translation Studies will find clear explanations to the general course of the field in Munday's (2001/2016) *Introducing Translation Studies*, but we will endeavour to provide introductions to the ideas necessary for our own purposes here as required.
2 Hasegawa (2012) explains that "language practice involves indexing a multiplicity of sociocultural significances (i.e., meanings), including the spatiotemporal locus of the communicative situation (i.e., *deixis, e.g., I, you, here, there, now, then*), personal characteristics of the speaker (age, sex, national origin), social identity (group membership), social acts (speech acts), social activities (sequences of social

acts, e.g., arguing, story-telling), and affective and epistemic (cognitive) stances."
We will return to the relevance of many of these same factors in the selection of
terms of address when translating from English into Korean and Japanese, in
Chapters 2 and 3.

3 A large family-owned business conglomerate in South Korea (OED, 2021).

4 Mentioned in passing earlier, the distinction between acceptability and adequacy
is made by Toury (1995/2012: 61), who suggests that translators will either be subject to norms of the target culture or language (an acceptable translation) or those
realised in the source text (an adequate translation).

2 Address Terms in the Japanese Translations of *The Hobbit, or There and Back Again* and *Harry Potter and the Philosopher's Stone*

In this chapter, we observe how address terms, including the second-person pronoun *you*, have been treated in published translations into Japanese of J.K. Rowling's (1997/2014) *Harry Potter and the Philosopher's Stone* (henceforth, *Harry Potter*) and J.R.R. Tolkien's (1937/2011) *The Hobbit, or There and Back Again* (henceforth, *The Hobbit*). The purpose of these case studies is to illustrate the heightened complexity of the repertoire of address terms in Japanese when compared to English.

2.1 Our Approach

We have attempted to combine a distant and close reading of the texts. The first stage was to identify all occurrences of address terms and second-person pronouns in the source text and to engage in a side-by-side reading with the target texts: (1) Matsuoka's (2019) translation of *Harry Potter* (henceforth, *Matsuoka's Harry Potter*), (2) Seta's (1979/2016) translation of *The Hobbit* (henceforth, *Seta's The Hobbit*), and (3) Yamamoto's (2012/2014) translation of *The Hobbit* (henceforth, *Yamamoto's The Hobbit*). References to the corpora in the discussion that follows are to these target texts.

The process of manually reviewing the corpora suggested certain trends and hypotheses that were then evaluated in a more quantitative manner. It is hoped that a combination of close and distant reading can help to catch phenomena that might be missed by one approach or the other. A purely quantitative analysis might be more likely to miss the choice in limited but significant circumstances of a particular address term, and a close reading of the corpora alone might be less likely to pick up more general trends in distribution.

2.2 Pronoun Omission

It is well-attested that pronouns are used less in Japanese than in English. Martin (1975/2004: 332) describes how Japanese speakers prefer to avoid direct pronominal reference, and to use a name and/or title or kin terms rather than second-person pronouns. Those familiar with the Japanese language will

DOI: 10.4324/9781003217466-2

be aware that the construction of a grammatical sentence in Japanese does not require the explicit inclusion of arguments (i.e., the expressions, such as a subject and/or object, that complete a predicate), unlike English where it is often assumed that a predicate must be accompanied by a subject as an absolute minimum. Although there certainly are scenarios where context makes the subject so obvious that it can readily be dropped even in English (for example, the question "coming tomorrow?" will generally be perfectly intelligible), this is a much more frequent phenomenon in Japanese, where it would appear more usual to drop nominal forms where contextual cues allow assumptions to be made as to the nouns that would fill these spaces. In the absence of other particular contextual or discursive factors indicating a different interpretation, the subject of a declarative sentence will be inferred to be the speaker, and that of an interrogative sentence as the addressee (Yonezawa 2021: 3). Incidentally, the frequency of second-person pronouns is low enough in Japanese that second-person pronouns are acquired by Japanese children at a later stage than their American counterparts (Clancy 1985: 457).

Shibatani (1990/2005: 360) confirms Martin's summary, and writes of the omission of nominal forms as the most pronounced demonstration of how Japanese is more elliptical than European languages in both speech and writing. Shibatani goes on to explain the heightened significance of context on the formation and comprehension of a given utterance in Japanese:

> Another factor that contributes to the seeming vagueness of Japanese is the high degree of contextual dependency that Japanese expressions show... a variety of contextual factors dictate the form of a Japanese expression, but the most striking structural feature relevant here is the absence of understood elements from the surface expression.
>
> (390–1)

At the highest level, the corpora bear out the idea that nominal forms are often elided in Japanese where they might be retained in English. *Matsuoka's Harry Potter* includes pronouns or other address terms in respect of 839 instances where they are used in the English version, and omits them in 867 instances (i.e., pronoun omission occurs in 49.18% of cases); *Seta's The Hobbit* includes pronouns or other address terms in respect of 546 occurrences in the original, and omits them in 666 instances (pronoun omission in 54.95% of cases); and *Yamamoto's The Hobbit* includes pronouns or other address terms in respect of 529 instances where they are used in the English version, and omits them in 683 instances (pronoun omission in 56.35% of cases). Three observations are particularly striking from these data: (1) pronoun omission is very common across the three translations to Japanese; (2) pronoun omission in all three translations clusters around the 50% mark, indicating that this may be a fairly regular phenomenon in literary translation from English to Japanese (although potentially restricted to or governed by factors such as genre, target readership age, etc.); and (3) although pronoun omission is very common, and similarly so in the three Japanese translations observed here, this constitutes a lower proportion of second-person references than in natural untranslated Japanese.

More involved discussion of the other options available to the translators will follow, but it is also worth noting right at the outset that the use of words that could be described as second-person pronouns without controversy form only a fraction of the address terms that are explicit at the surface level. *Matsuoka's Harry Potter* contains 390 second-person pronouns, of the 839 instances where some address term is explicit (that is to say, 46.48% of overt address terms were clear second-person pronouns). As *you* (or variations such as *your*) appear 1,057 times in the corpus for *Harry Potter*, this marks a significant reduction in the use of second-person pronouns in translation from English to Japanese. The results are similar with the two Japanese translations of *The Hobbit*: Seta's version had 302 non-controversial second-person pronouns of 546 total overt address terms (55.31%); Yamamoto's version had 305 clear second-person pronouns of 529 total overt address terms (57.66%) (there were 997 appearances of *you* and its relatives in the English corpus for *The Hobbit*).

Even if it has been observed that second-person pronouns only make up around half of all overt references to the second-person, these pronouns seem to be much more commonly distributed than in natural untranslated Japanese; Martin (1975/2004: 1075), for example, refers to a study in which it was found that only 0.28% of overt references in spoken Japanese to the second-person were pronouns (v. 6, pp. 202–3 of vol. 6 of *Kōza gendai-go*). It is very possible that this is an artefact of the translation process, with translators feeling a certain traction to reflect not only what is said in the source text, but also the way that it is said.

The idea that translation can have an impact on language is well-attested. In the context of literary translation in Japan, Mizuno (2012/2013) describes how the 1885 text *Keishidan* (a translation of Bulwer-Lytton's *Kenelm Chillingly*) played a key role in the development of conscious translation strategies in Japan. Mizuno provides an illustrative excerpt from the translator's preface to that text in which the translator (presumed to be Asahina Chisen) stresses the importance of paying attention to form, as well as content, and describes having tried to retain the formal features of the original as much as possible in the target text without concern for the violation of target-language conventions (104–5).

From the perspective of polysystem theory (discussed in Chapter 1), this can be seen as an expression of a preference for translation based around adequacy with respect to the source text, rather than acceptability to the target culture. Yanabu's (1982/2004) discussion of the Japanese words *kare* and *kanojo*, commonly described as third-person pronouns equivalent to *he* and *she*, sheds light on how powerful the force exerted by a source language can be on the style of the target text, and the traction this can exert over time on the source language more generally. Yanabu describes how *kare* was originally a demonstrative pronoun, referring to a thing or person (but more commonly a thing) external to both speaker and listener, with similar nuance to the distal *a* in the Japanese language's distinction between the proximal-mesial-distal pronominal prefixes *ko-so-a*. Noting the difference between the pronominal systems in European languages and Japanese, Yanabu goes so far as to say the following:

> The Japanese language did not originally have third-person pronouns, and I am of the opinion that even today it can be said that they do not exist in Japanese…
>
> The development of the modern meaning of the word *kare* is primarily a result of its use in translation.
>
> (trans. Andre Hang, provided in Levy 2011: 62–4)

Yanabu contrasts the different systems of European languages and of Japanese by explaining that the primary role of third person pronouns in the former is to explicitly articulate a grammatical subject, which is a formal require-ment in such languages, but that in Japanese a subject is generally omitted where it can be understood from the context. Yanabu notes, however, that the words *kare* and *kanojo* "gradually invaded written Japanese, and it became more common to write sentences in which the subject of the action was made explicit" (66–7).

Yanabu confirms the significant impact that translation can have on the language of the target text, as well as the target language more generally. However, the assumption that Japanese would have a similar pronominal system to English or other European languages is one that needs to be tested, rather than assumed as a matter of course. The reader is sure to have noted the many references in our own case study to "clear second-person pronouns" or "uncontroversial second-person pronouns." This will be discussed fur-ther in due course, but is based on the fact that many of the terms seemingly used to translate *you* into Japanese in the texts analysed are different to *you* in important ways. To assume that they are second-person pronouns simply because a translator has used them to translate *you* would be to fall into the trap that we have just warned against. Yanabu stresses that, even though the Japanese language has been transformed by the importance of transla-tion (from the perspective of polysystem theory, this would be an instance of translation as a central or primary system exerting its influence on native literature as a periphery or secondary system) – which has changed the use of *kare* and *kanojo*, as well as increasing the frequency of explicit subjects in Japanese more generally – *kare* and *kanojo* in Japanese are still different to *he* and *she* in English. Yanabu notes that *kare* and *kanojo* remain connected to the speaker's position. He also states that *kare* and *kanojo* "are pronouns, but at the same time resemble proper nouns. Moreover they are now used to refer to something that has a positive value. Namely, young people frequently use "your *kanojo*" and "my *kare*" to refer to their lovers, boyfriends or girlfriends" (Levy 2011: 70). Second-person references are similarly far from objective in Japanese, and their use cannot be divorced from a number of pragmatic factors.

Another point is that a grammatical subject will tend to be omitted in Japanese except when specifically necessary. If that is correct, one would hope to be able to identify some motivation behind the inclusion of a grammatical subject in Japanese in any given instance. With translation, of course, the very existence of *you* in the source text could itself be seen as such motivation, with a translator wanting to render a target text with maximal adequacy, as just discussed. However, we have also seen that in our own case studies, clear second-person pronouns are only used in the Japanese text around half the time that *you* (or variants thereof) appear in the source texts. Accordingly, further analysis might be required as to the other factors underlying these translation decisions. Incidentally, where Yanabu has referred to subjects, for our purposes it is perhaps more helpful to think of a preference for the omission of pronouns more generally.

2.3 Indexical Meaning

In the previous section, it was observed that the terms *kare* and *kanojo* appear to play the role of both pronoun and proper noun, and that the use of both third- and second-person pronouns in Japanese is inextricably tied to pragmatic factors such as the position of the speaker. That second-person pronouns in Japanese carry a more diverse range of meanings than the *you* of English is perhaps best shown in the much wider pool of available terms. English tends to require overt arguments to accompany a given predicate, and pronouns such as *you* allow such a slot to be filled without adding unnecessary semantic baggage; Japanese, which does not require overt arguments, and which has in fact has been described as preferring to avoid overt pronominal reference, instead has a spectrum of alternatives, the use of which is determined by pragmatic factors.

In the first chapter, we referred to Hasegawa's (2012: 56–9) discussion of the difficulties that arise in translation between English and Japanese as a result of Japanese encoding "too much" indexical meaning. It might be beneficial to look a little closer at this argument. Hasegawa defines indexicality as follows (herself referring to Lyons 1977):

[A] sign A indexes information C when the occurrence of A can imply the presence or existence of C (Lyons 1977: 106)… the presence of *ore* implies that the speaker is male, as well as that the speech situation is casual, or, if the speaker is in fact a woman, that the speech is in a dialect such as that of Saitama prefecture, where *ore* is used by both sexes.

(Hasegawa 2012: 56–7)

Hasegawa also notes an overlap here with "expressive meaning," taken to refer to the attitudes, beliefs, and/or emotions of the speaker. Two expressions that are synonymous with respect to their propositional meaning can carry very different expressive meaning (50). Let us look at some of the second-person references used in our case studies to illustrate these ideas. Table 2.1 provides some basic information about second-person pronouns used in *Yamamoto's The Hobbit*, based on their entries in the dictionary *Reikai shinkokugo jiten* (2006). As noted by Yonezawa (2021: 6) with respect specifically to *anata*, the information provided by dictionaries on second-person pronouns can be somewhat vague. Nonetheless, we hope that this will illustrate what are seen to be some of the crucial distinctions, and serve as a starting point for the discussion that follows.

This is neither an exhaustive list of the range of second-person pronouns available in Japanese, nor even of all of those used in the three corpora. Nevertheless, it should be clear from Table 2.1 that there are a much wider range of second-person pronouns available in Japanese than in English, and that that even extremely concise dictionary entries with respect to these pronouns frequently refer to the importance of the respective social positions of the speaker and addressee. For example, certain pronouns are described as being for use to one's equal or inferior. The matter is further complicated by the fact that Japanese second-person pronouns are encoded for number. Most of those listed in Table 2.1 are singular by default, while *shokun* (諸君) is plural. Those second-person pronouns that are singular by default can be made plural by the addition of a plural-marking suffix. Much like the pronouns themselves, however, these suffixes also carry varied pragmatic meanings. The plural-marking suffixes that appear in *Yamamoto's The Hobbit*, affixed to the clear second-person pronouns listed in Table 2.1, are listed in Table 2.2. Because of the pragmatic meanings associated with these suffixes, and the fact that they are therefore not distributed randomly with any of the pronouns in Table 2.1, the suffixes are listed together with those second-person pronouns to which they are appended in the text. It should also be noted that these are only the plural-marking suffixes that appear in *Yamamoto's The Hobbit* with the clear second-person pronouns listed in Table 2.1; there are other plural-marking pronouns that appear in the text with other nominal forms.

Plural-marking in Japanese is also different to that of English in that adding a plural-marking suffix to a nominal in Japanese has the meaning less of marking that nominal as itself plural as of referring to a group that includes that nominal (and may or may not include more than one of the nominal's referents). This complicates the analysis of second-person references used in the corpora because it can be unclear who exactly is being addressed as the principal, and who is included in the group with that principal addressee.

Table 2.1 A conservative list of second-person pronouns used in *Yamamoto's The Hobbit*

Japanese	Romanisation	Information provided in *Reikai shinkokugo jiten5*
あなた	*anata*	(Pronoun) Used to refer to one's counterpart. See also *kimi*. Note: Used with counterparts who are one's equal or inferior. Usually written in hiragana. Corresponds to the kanji 貴方. Where the counterpart is female, can also be written as 貴女.
あんた	*anta*	(Pronoun) A colloquial way of saying *anata*.
おまえ	*omae*	Kanji: お前. (Pronoun) Used to address one's equals or one's inferiors.
お前	*omae*	[See *omae* as おまえ. Note, however, the appearance of this word as both おまえ and お前 in the text (i.e., an orthographic difference).]
そなた	*sonata*	(Pronoun) 1. *socchi* (see *sochira*). 2. *Kimi, omae*. An archaic way of saying both (1) and (2).
君	*kimi*	Kanji: 君. 1. (Noun) A respectful term for a lord or a king. 2. (Pronoun) Used to address a counterpart who is one's equal or inferior. Mainly used by men.
諸君	*shokun*	Kanji: 諸君.(Pronoun) Used to address a large group of people who are one's equals or inferiors, with an attitude of respect and friendliness.
貴殿	*kiden*	Kanji: 貴殿. (Pronoun) Used to address one's counterpart. Nuance: Used by men to refer to men who are their equals or inferiors. Used in letters and official documents.
てめえ	*temē*	Kanji: 手前. (Pronoun) A coarser way of saying *omae*.
汝	*nanji*	Kanji: 汝. (Pronoun) An archaic way of saying *omae*.
そちら	*sochira*	(Pronoun) 1. Near the listener. Also used to refer to a thing that is near the listener. 2. Used to refer to one's counterpart or a person close to that counterpart. *Sochira* has the same meaning as *socchi*, but is more polite.
そちら側	*sochiragawa*	[See *sochira*. Information on the suffix *gawa* follows.] (Suffix) In the direction or area of the thing to which it is affixed.
貴公	*kikō*	Kanji: 貴公. (Pronoun) An archaic way of saying *kimi*. Originally used to address one's superiors.

Table 2.2 Pluralising suffixes that attach to second-person pronouns in *Yamamoto's
The Hobbit*

Japanese	Romanisation	Definition in 例解新国語辞典, and an English explanation
あなたがた	anatagata	[See *anata* in Table 2.1. Information on the suffix *gata* follows.] Kanji: 方. (Suffix) Indicates reference to two or more people, with an attitude of respect.
あんたら	antara	[See *anta* in Table 2.1. Information on the suffix *ra* follows.] 1. Affixed to words that refer to people, indicating plurality. Used with people who are one's peers or inferiors. 2. Used when referring to a group, attaching to the name of a person taken to be the principal of that group as an abbreviation. 3. Affixed to the demonstrative pronouns *kore-sore-are* to indicate plurality. Also affixed to *koko-soko-asoko-doko* to indicate proximity to the area denoted thereby.
お前ら	omaera	[See *omae* in Table 2.1 and *antara* in this table for information on the suffix *ra*.]
君たち	kimitachi	[see *kimi* in Table 2.1. Information on the suffix *tachi* follows.] Kanji: 等.(Suffix) Affixed to words that refer to people to indicate plurality.
貴殿ら	kidenra	[see *kiden* in Table 2.1 and *antara* in this table for information on the suffix *ra*.]
てめえら	temēra	[See *temē* in Table 2.1 and *antara* in this table for information on the suffix *ra*.]

2.4 Alternatives to Second-Person Pronouns

That pronoun omission is both possible and common in Japanese (both natural Japanese and the translated case studies) has been discussed. But we
should also briefly touch on the alternatives noted in the passage quoted from
Martin (1975/2004: 332): name and/or title, kin terms, and exaltation. We will
look at each of these options now, before turning to other common strategies
for translating references to the second person.

2.4.1 Name and/or Title

The use of a name might at first appear easy to grasp for someone coming
from an English-speaking background, where people's names are commonly
used to address them. In English, it would be highly unusual for a name to be
used to refer to one's addressee as the argument of a predicate; where a name

is used, it would be assumed to be playing the role of a third-person reference. The following examples are all grammatical only where the name "John" is assumed to refer to some third person, rather than the speaker or addressee (or, if John is the addressee, this would be a rhetorical device for emphasis, and grammatically speaking, one would interpret "John" as a third person reference):

(1)
a.   John is here.
b.   Is John here?
c.   I see John.
d.   I'm giving this to John.

Were John the addressee, one would restructure the examples, possibly along the following lines:

(2)
a.   John, you're here.
b.   Are you here, John?
c.   I see you, John.
d.   I'm giving this to you, John.

Note that in all of these examples, a grammatical utterance would also remain if "John" were to be removed. The role of the name in these examples cannot be satisfactorily analysed as that of an argument accompanying the predicate; instead, this is a pure term of address, used to clarify to whom one is speaking (i.e., who *you* refers to). This distinction is important because Japanese also commonly introduces nouns as so-called themes – a position for which it can be difficult to find analogues in European languages – and in the discussion that follows we should be careful as to whether a nominal form is playing the role of subject grammatically, even if logically we know that its referent is the agent of the action denoted by the predicate.

In any case, and in contrast to English, grammatical Japanese utterances can be formed that use the addressee's name and/or title in the position of an argument. Although it must be said that such structures are exceptionally rare in the case study corpora, the following is an example from *Harry* Potter and *Matsuoka's Harry Potter* (we have underlined the name in the Japanese text, together with the particle that marks it as a grammatical subject):

(3)
[Harry Potter to Hagrid]

Hagrid, he'd have found out somehow, this is Voldemort we're talking about, he'd have found out even if you hadn't told him.

(Harry Potter: 326)

ハグリッド、あいつはどう見つけだしていたよ。相手はヴォルデモー
トだもの。<u>ハグリッドが</u>何も言わなくたって、どうせ見つけていた
さ

(Matsuoka's Harry Potter: 468)

It is likely that part of the explanation for why the inclusion of the addressee's name as an overt subject here (rather than omitted, which should be understood as the general preference, in the absence of a particular motivation for inclusion, as discussed earlier in this chapter) is the change of subject mid-sentence – Voldemort is the subject of the following clause, and has been fronted as a theme by the preceding sentence, so the inclusion of the overt second-person reference helps to clarify this shift. In any case, this option remains available in Japanese, unlike English.

More generally, the use of names and/or titles for second-person reference is very common across the case study corpora. In *Matsuoka's Harry Potter*, for example, there are forty-seven instances where the title *sensei* (先生) is used for overt second-person reference. Two examples are presented here – one in which the title accompanies a name, and one in which the title is used in isolation (the overt second-person references have been underlined):

(4)
[Professor Dumbledore to Professor McGonagall]
Fancy seeing you here, Professor McGonagall.

(Harry Potter: 10)

<u>マクゴナガル先生、</u>こんな所で奇遇じゃのう

(Matsuoka's Harry Potter: 19)

(5)
[Professor McGonagall to Professor Dumbledore]
But you're different.

(Harry Potter: 12)

だって、<u>先生</u>はみんなとは違います。

(Matsuoka's Harry Potter: 22)

Using a name without a title (referred to as *yobisute* (呼び捨て) in Japanese) is considered impolite, and so tends to only be used towards intimate addressees, or where the addressee is socially inferior to the speaker. This is quite common in *Matsuoka's Harry Potter*, where there are 290 instances of *yobisute*. These are found frequently in casual conversation, in particular among the children at Hogwarts (in terms of frequency, it is conversations among Harry Potter, Hermione Granger, and Ron Weasley that the reader is exposed to the most), between Hagrid and Harry, Hermione, and Ron, and when Mrs Weasley addresses her children. Of the examples just listed, the use of *yobisute* by children towards Hagrid, an adult man, is striking. This phenomenon is notably also present in the Korean translation of *Harry Potter*, discussed in Chapter 3. It is possible that Harry, Ron, and Hermione addressing this character simply as Hagrid (ハヽグリッド) reflects not only the intimate relationship that develops between those three children and the Hogwarts groundskeeper, but also the idea that Hagrid is somehow excluded from normal society and its normal rules. The fact that Harry addresses Hagrid in this fashion even at their first meeting (despite also using *anata*) makes this latter interpretation, that Hagrid is somehow a unique individual to whom normal rules don't apply, appear more likely.

Yobisute is also not uncommon in *Matsuoka's Harry Potter* in more formal classroom occasions, where teachers are addressing students. For the purposes of the *yobisute* tally, we did not count instances where English-language titles such as *miss* or *mister* were transliterated into Japanese; even though a strict analysis could treat these as names without a title suffix of any kind, common sense dictated that the retention of an English-language title (as a prefix) lead to its omission from any count of *yobisute*.

Yobisute is less common in both of the Japanese translations of *The Hobbit*. We counted sixty-eight instances of *yobisute* in *Yamamoto's The Hobbit* and seventy-eight instances in *Seta's The Hobbit*. Some borderline cases were eliminated from these tallies because, despite the absence of any honorific suffix, formal qualifiers relating to an addressee's ancestry preceded their name. A typical example is provided here:

(6)
[Röac (a thrush) to Thorin and Balin]
O Thorin son of Thrain, and Balin son of Fundin...

(The Hobbit: 288)

おお、スラインのむすこ、トーリンよ。また、フンディンのむすこ
バーリンよ。

(Seta's The Hobbit, vol. 2: 176)

This example also contains another element that distinguishes many of the instances of *yobisute* in both translations of *The Hobbit*, namely the presence of vocative particles (in this case *yo* (よ), but one also finds *ya* (や)). It is possible that the use of these particles obviates, to a certain extent, the usual concerns that would be associated with the absence of any kind of honorific suffix or title, given that these vocative particles have something of a poetic or archaic sense to them, setting the expressions apart from everyday speech.

Occasionally the use of *yobisute* may be an attempt to reflect marked differences in the formality of address used in the English text. The following example from both translations of *The Hobbit* may be illustrative of this.

(7)
[Thorin, leader of the dwarves, to Gandalf, Bilbo, and the other dwarves]
Gandalf, dwarves, and Mr. Baggins!

(*The Hobbit*: 20)

ガンダルフ、ドワーフたち、そしてバギンズどの。
(*Yamamoto's The Hobbit*, vol. 1: 32)

ガンダルフよ、ドワーフたちよ、またバギンズどのよ。
(*Seta's The Hobbit*, vol. 1: 42)

Here, it can be seen that the honorific suffix *dono* (どの) is used in both translations for "Mr. Baggins," but Gandalf's name is used without any such suffix or title. This may have been motivated by a desire to mark the absence for "Mr" with respect to Gandalf in the original text, as honorific suffixes are sometimes added in the translations even where individuals are not addressed as "Mr" or the like in the source text. The following is a typical example.

(8)
[Bilbo to Bard, hero of the Lake-Men]
My dear Bard!

(*The Hobbit*: 302)

これはしたり、バルドどの！
(*Seta's The Hobbit*, vol. 2: 201)

Thus, it would appear that the translators have made judgments as to whether to include an honorific suffix on the basis of the perceived relationship between the speaker and addressee, and their expectations as to what would be most appropriate for such a relationship.

2.4.2 Kin Terms

The use of kin terms is relatively simple to understand, with the proviso that they can also be used in the positions of arguments with respect to the predicate, just like names and/or titles, as discussed earlier. Kin terms can be used to address non-relatives as well as actual relatives, in which case an approximation is made as to the family position that person might occupy were they in the speaker's family (based principally on age and sex). This phenomenon is not particularly common in the case study translations, but the following example illustrates the availability of this option.

(9)
[Piers, a child, to Vernon Dursley, the father of Piers' friend Dudley]
MR DURSLEY!

(*Harry Potter*: 29)

ダーズリーおじさん！

(*Matsuoka's Harry Potter*: 47)

Matsuoka has Piers refer to Mr Dursley as uncle Dursley because Mr Dursley is a man of similar age to his own father.

2.4.3 Subject-Exalting Predicates

Martin's mention to exaltation as an alternative to the use of pronouns refers to subject-exalting or object-exalting predicate forms. Where a subject-exalting a form of predicate is used, it becomes clear that the predicate is taking a second-person subject. There are a range of subject-exalting structures available (for a fuller explanation, see Martin 1975/2004: 336–8); Table 2.3 provides a summary of the normal patters for subject exaltation on the basis of that text. Please note, however, that this is far from an exhaustive list of available structures and that, in particular, there exist many verbs that have subject-exalting euphemistic synonyms (which are subject-exalting as a basic rule, and therefore do not require restructuring along the lines set out in Table 2.3).

Table 2.3 Subject-exalting predicate formation

Predicate type	Example of basic form	Example of subject-exalting form
Verb	*yobu* 呼ぶ	*o-yobi ni naru* お呼びになる
Verbal noun	*sōdan suru* 相談	*go-sōdan ni naru* ご相談になる
Adjective	*isogashī* 忙しい	(o-)isogashikute irassharu (お)忙しくていらっしゃる
Adjectival noun	*genki da* 元気だ	(o-)genki de irassharu (お)元気でいらっしゃる
Precopular noun	*byōki da* 病気だ	(go-)byōki de irassharu (ご)病気でいらっしゃる
Noun	*sensei da* 先生だ	Sensei de irassharu 先生でいらっしゃる

Some examples from the corpora follow (with the subject-exalting predicates underlined):

(10)
[Professor McGonagall to Professor Dumbledore]
How did you know it was me?

(Harry Potter: 10)

どうしてわたくし私だと<u>お分りになりました</u>の？

(Matsuoka's Harry Potter: 20)

(11)
[The narrator to the reader(s)]
If you have ever seen a dragon in a pinch, you will realize that this was only poetical exaggeration applied to any hobbit, even to Old Took's great-grand-uncle Bullroarer, who was so huge (for a hobbit) that he could ride a horse.

(The Hobbit: 21)

もしも読者の皆さんが"窮地に立ったドラゴン"なるのを一度でも<u>ご
らんになった</u>ことがおありなら、この言葉をホビットにあてはめる
ことが、いかに詩的に誇張下表現であるかということが、たちどこ
ろに<u>お分りになる</u>でしょう。

(Yamamoto's The Hobbit, vol. 1: 34)

(12)
[Bilbo to Gandalf]
If you have a pipe about you, sit down and have a fill of mine!

(The Hobbit: 6)

どうです、パイプを<u>おもちなら</u>、ここにすわって、わたしのきざみ
を<u>おすいなさい</u>。

(Seta's The Hobbit, vol. 1: 17)

Prima facie, especially from the perspective of an English-speaker, this could be taken as removing the need for an overt second-person pronoun or other term of address – that is to say, as fulfilling the role of a second-person pronoun or other address term and making their appearance redundant. But the issue is somewhat more complex than that. For example, it is perfectly possible for a subject-exalting predicate to accompany a second-person pronoun or other address term. The following example could almost be considered an embarrassment of riches when it comes to second-person reference in Japanese, with a name and title, a second-person pronoun, and a subject-exalting predicate (example 11 also includes an overt reference to the reader as subject, as well as subject-exalting predicates).

(13)
[Ollivander, an elderly man who sells magic wands, to Harry Potter]
I think we must expect great things form you, Mr Potter…

(Harry Potter: 92)

<u>ポッターさん</u>、<u>あなたは</u>きっと偉大なことを<u>なさる</u>に違いない…

(Matsuoka's Harry Potter: 136)

It is also by no means obligatory for a predicate taking a second-person sub-ject to be subject-exalting. The determination of whether to use a subject-exalting predicate should perhaps be considered more one of agreement than as simply one either/or option for marking a second-person subject. There are plenty of cases in which a predicate that takes a second-person subject is not a subject-exalting form (if the subject is a close friend, for example, and so does not require exaltation) and, as example 13 shows, there can also be utterances in which multiple overt references mark the second-person subject.

2.4.4 Subject-Humbling Predicates

Martin (1975/2004: 342–5) refers to object exaltation, but his description of the uses of these forms reveal that it may be better to refer to subject-humbling predicates (or a similar term), because these predicates need not exalt the object of the predicate itself, but rather express a humbling of the speaker relative to a direct object, an adjunct other than the subject or object, an embedded genitive (that may be overt or implied), an unmentioned bene-ficiary of the action, or even simply to show general humility. The standard structure for rendering a predicate into this subject-humbling form is set out in Table 2.4 (although, note that subject-humbling euphemistic synonyms also exist).

An example from the case studies is provided in the following example (with the subject-humbling predicate underlined).

(14)
[Gandalf to Beorn]
We were crossing by the High Pass that should have brought us to the road that lies to the south of your country, when we were attacked by the evil goblins – as I was about to tell you.

(The Hobbit: 137)

わしらは、おおとうげ大峠を超えて、ここからはるか南にあたる道に出ようと思っていたところ、はからずもゴブリンのあくとう悪党どもにおそわれたのじゃ。いまそれを<u>お話しよう</u>としておったところです。

(Seta's The Hobbit, vol. 1: 239)

Table 2.4 Subject-humbling predicate formation

Predicate type	Example of basic form	Example of subject-exalting form
Verb	*yobu* 呼ぶ	*o-yobi suru* お呼びする
Verbal noun	*sōdan suru* 相談する	*go-sōdan suru* ご相談する

The use of the subject-humbling form implies an exalted counterpart to the speaker, which will generally be interpreted as the second person (in example 14, this makes it clear that it is to Beorn that Gandalf says he was about to tell this information).

2.4.5 *Favours*

Auxiliary verbs relating to the giving and receiving of favours (i.e., the action denoted by the predicate being performed on behalf of someone) can also serve to provide an indication of person. Example 15 shows the auxiliary verb *ageru* used to indicate that the action expressed by the predicate *okosu* is performed as a favour. In the context of the discussion, the addressee can be easily retrieved as the beneficiary of this action. Although grammatically speaking it is not necessary for the beneficiary to be the object of the action (Bilbo could just as easily wake someone else up on Bombur's behalf, although in that case one would expect some contextual or overt evidence to suggest such an interpretation), from the perspective of a translator, such structures provide a potential strategy for conveying a sense of the second person in a natural manner.

> (15)
> [Bilbo Baggins to Bombur]
> I will wake you at midnight, and you can wake the next watchman.
> (*The Hobbit*: 300)

> 真夜中になったら、おこしてあげよう。そうしたらあんたが、次の
> 番の人をおこせばいい。
> (*Seta's The Hobbit*, vol. 2: 196–7)

2.4.6 **Minasan, *Reflexive Pronouns, and Quantity Nominals***

Let us now look at three other strategies commonly used in the case studies to translate references to the second person: the use of *minasan*, of reflexive pronouns, and of quantity nominals. We have decided not to treat m*inasan* (which appears most commonly as みなさん in the case studies, but also occasionally as 皆さん in *Yamamoto's The Hobbit*, and has a similar meaning to "everyone") as an uncontroversial second-person pronoun. This is because, although the context can make it clear that the addressee is included within the referent of *minasan* (that the addressees are included within, or constitute the entire, referent), this can also refer to the third person (much like "everyone" in English) or even more generally to "everyone" as a group of people, which may or may not include the speaker and/or the addressee(s). The following examples are illustrative of the scope for interpretation here (examples 16 and 17 represent consecutive utterances within the same dialogue).

(16)
[Bilbo, to the Dwarves]
I will give you a good breakfast before you go.

(*The Hobbit*: 31)

みなさんのおたちの前に、ちょっとした朝ごはんをさしあげたいのですが…

(*Seta's The Hobbit*, vol. 1: 61)

(17)
[Thorin, responding to Bilbo]
Before *we* go, I suppose you mean,

(*The Hobbit*: 31)

みなさんとは、自分も入れて、そういったのじゃろうな。

(*Seta's The Hobbit*, vol. 1: 61)

In the Japanese version in *Seta's The Hobbit*, Bilbo refers to "everyone's departure" (みなさんのおたち), and Thorin tries to clarify that Bilbo is including himself in this "everyone."

Matsuoka's Harry Potter includes ten instances where *minasan* is used to refer to the second person, *Seta's The Hobbit* includes twenty-four instances where *minasan* is used to refer to the second person and three instances where *minasama* (a more polite version of the same, with the suffix *sama* instead of *san*) is used to refer to the second person, and *Yamamoto's The Hobbit* includes twenty-nine instances where *minasan* is used to refer to the second person and two instances where *minasama* is used to refer to the second person.

The use of reflexive pronouns is also observed in all three of the translations as a strategy for translating references to the second person. The reflexive pronoun *jibun* (自分) is used to refer to the second person eleven times in *Matsuoka's Harry Potter*, five times in *Yamamoto's The Hobbit*, and five times in *Seta's The Hobbit*. Although the reflexive pronoun *jibun* is sometimes used where the source texts simply have the second-person pronoun *you* (i.e., there is no overt reflexive in the English), the distribution of *jibun* in the corpora is restricted to instances where one would expect to find a reflexive pronoun – that is to say it is either used in the position of an object or adjunct to a predicate where the second person is also the subject, or to the subject of the predicate in a subordinate clause where the second person is the subject of the main predicate (even if the second-person subject of the predicate in question is not itself overt). Examples of this follow:.

(18)
[Hagrid to Harry Potter]
Yeh don't know what yeh *are*?

(Harry Potter: 54)

おまえさんは、自分が**何者なのか**知らんのだな？

(Matsuoka's Harry Potter: 80)

(19)
[Gandalf to Thorin]
You will get there in a few days now, if we're lucky, and find out all about it.

(The Hobbit: 51)

運がよけりゃ、数日もすればそこに到着して、自分の目で見られるよ。

(Yamamoto's The Hobbit, vol. 1: 80)

(20)
[Bilbo to himself]
Bilbo, you were a fool; you walked right in and put your foot in it.

(The Hobbit: 22)

ビルボ、おまえはばか者だぞ。ちゃんと自分の分を守っていればよかったのに！

(Seta's The Hobbit, vol. 1: 45–6)

Finally, let us turn to quantity nominals. For our purposes the discussion will be restricted to the counting of people, rather than the full spectrum of all countable nouns. The particular quantity nominals relevant to the corpora are *futari* (二人; "two people") and *sannin* (三人; "three people"). Both quantity nominals can be analysed as the combination of a numeral (*futa* or *san*) with a counter (*ri* is an alternate form of *nin*, the counter for people).

Of particular interest with respect to the quantity nominals is the fact that they can fulfil a range of roles within a given utterance. Martin (1974/2004: 777) explains that a number (the term he uses to refer to the combination of a numeral and a counter) "can be used as a pure noun… or predicated by some form of the copula; by conversion of the copula to nó, the number can be adnominalized; and it can be directly adverbialized – i.e., used as an adverb – with or without focus (mó, wá, etc.) or restrictive (⁻gúrai, ⁻dake, etc.) or similar element (⁻zútú "each")." This approach to the translation of second-person references is more common in *Matsuoka's Harry Potter*, where there are eighteen such uses of *futari*, and five uses of *sannin*. There are only three instances of *futari* used for second-person reference in *Yamamoto's The Hobbit*, and no such instances in *Seta's The Hobbit*. Neither Japanese translation of *The Hobbit* includes any occurrences of *sannin* for second-person reference. Some representative examples follow:.

(21)
[Vernon Dursley to Harry Potter and Dudley Dursley]
Get out, both of you,

(*Harry Potter*: 38)

あっちへ行け！二人ともだ

(*Matsuoka's Harry Potter*: 59)

(22)
[Hagrid to Harry Potter]
All anyone knows is, he turned up in the village where you was all living, on Hallowe'en ten years ago.

(*Harry Potter*: 49–60)

分かっているのは、十年前のハロウィーンに、おまえさんたち三人が住んでいた村にあやつがあらわ現れたってことだけだ。

(*Matsuoka's Harry Potter*: 89)

(23)
[Thorin to Bilbo Baggins and Balin]
Up you two get, and off we go!

(*The Hobbit*: 35)

さあ二人とも馬にのって。出発だ！

(*Yamamoto's The Hobbit*, vol. 1: 56)

(24)
[Beorn to Oin and Gloin]
Come along, you two, and sit down!

(*The Hobbit*: 140)

君たち二人とも、さあさ、こっちにきて座りなさい。

(*Yamamoto's The Hobbit*, vol. 1: 219)

Pragmatically, using these quantity nominals avoids the harshness of more direct second-person pronouns. However, the potential to use quantity nominals alongside a second-person pronoun (examples 22 and 24, for instance) shows that they can fulfil a different grammatical role.

2.5 The Distribution of Particular Second-Person Pronouns

The discussion in the previous section has considered the options available to a translator from English to Japanese when treating second-person reference. A range of alternatives to second-person pronouns has been shown, not least of which is omission of any overt second-person reference at all. It was also shown that where second-person pronouns are used in Japanese, there is a much broader inventory available than in English, and it was noted that pragmatic factors play a role in the selection of items from this inventory. In this section, we will take a closer look at the distribution of some of these pronouns. Because of the prohibitive volume of options, this description does not pretend to be exhaustive, providing neither a complete analysis of all the factors relevant to a particular pronoun nor an analysis of every second-person pronoun used in the corpora. Nonetheless, we hope to highlight some of the key factors of relevance to the more common second-person pronouns *kimi*, *anata*, and *omae*, as well as discussing the role that rarer alternatives can play in providing a distinctive voice to particular characters.

2.5.1 Kimi, Anata, *and* Omae

In the tables in this section, a superscript P is appended to an addressee where that addressee is only referred to by the given speaker with the pluralised form of in the pronoun in question. As has been noted earlier in this chapter, the plural-marking suffixes in Japanese act in a manner that refers to a group including the referent of the noun to which they are attached, rather than to a group of the referents of that noun (e.g., the phrase *sensei-tachi* refers to a group including a single individual referred to as *sensei*, although of course there could be multiple people capable of being referred to as *sensei* within that group). This is relevant because, for example, where the ghost Peeves addresses a group that includes Hermione Granger with a pluralised form of *kimi*, it is not clear whether Peeves would refer to Hermione Granger as an individual with *kimi*.

Tables 2.5 to 2.7 set out who uses *kimi*, and to whom, in the corpora.

The reader may recall the basic definition from Table 2.1 of *kimi* as a pronoun used primarily by men to refer to an equal or inferior. What can our corpora tell us about the use of *kimi*? Let us look first at this most basic statement about gender and relative social status.

There is only one clear instance of a female speaker using *kimi* in *Matsuoka's Harry Potter*. This is Madam Pince, in the following single example:

(25)
[Madam Pince to Harry Potter]
What are you looking for, boy?

(*Harry Potter*: 212)

君、何を探しているの？

(*Matsuoka's Harry Potter*: 302)

Table 2.5 Speaker and addressee where *kimi* is used in *Matsuoka's Harry Potter*

Speaker	Addressee
Professor Dumbledore	Harry Potter
	All Hogwarts students
Harry Potter	Dudley Dursley (uncle)
	Neville Longbottom
	Ron Weasley
	Hermione Granger
Professor Quirrell	Harry Potter
	Professor Snape
Draco Malfoy	Harry Potter
	Neville Longbottom
	Ron Weasley
Percy Weasley	Harry Potter
Fred Weasley	Harry Potter
	Percy Weasley (older brother)
George Weasley	Harry Potter
	Percy Weasley (older brother)
Neville Longbottom	Harry Potter
	Draco Malfoy
	Ron Weasley
	Hermione Granger[P]
Ron Weasley	Harry Potter
	Draco Malfoy
	Neville Longbottom
	Hermione Granger
	Nearly Headless Nick
Ghost (unnamed character)	New first-year students at Hogwarts
The sorting hat	Harry Potter
	Hogwarts students (in song) [singular]
Peeves	Harry Potter[P]
	Neville Longbottom[P]
	Ron Weasley[P]
	Hermione Granger[P]
Professor Snape	Harry Potter
Professor Flitwick	Harry Potter
	Draco Malfoy[P]
	Ron Weasley[P]
Oliver Wood	Harry Potter
Madam Pince	Harry Potter
Charlie Weasley	Ron Weasley
Bane (centaur)	Firenze (centaur)
Firenze (centaur)	Harry Potter
Riddle left by Professor Snape	Anyone who were to read the riddle

Table 2.6 Speaker and addressee where *kimi* is used in *Yamamoto's The Hobbit*

Speaker	Addressee
Bilbo Baggins	The dwarves[P]
	Fili[P]
	Kili[P]
	Bombur
	Forest elves[P]
Gandalf	Bilbo Baggins
	The dwarves[P]
Dwalin	Bilbo Baggins
The dwarves	Bombur
Thorin	Bilbo Baggins
	The dwarves[P]
	Bombur
Beorn	Bilbo[P]
	Gandalf
	Balin[P]
	Dwalin[P]
	Thorin
	Dori[P]
Bombur	Bilbo Baggins
The elf-king	Bilbo Baggins
	Gandalf
Galion	Forest elves
Lake-men	Bilbo Baggins
	Other lake-men
Bard	Bilbo Baggins

Table 2.7 Speaker and addressee where *kimi* is used in *Seta's The Hobbit*

Speaker	Addressee
Gandalf	Dori
Balin	Bilbo

Three other speakers could potentially be interpreted as without gender in the source text, and use *kimi* in *Matsuoka's Harry Potter*, although for at least two of these an interpretation as male is probably more likely: an unnamed ghost, the sorting hat, and a riddle left by Professor Snape, but purporting to speak on behalf of an assortment of potions. The unnamed ghost is described as wearing a ruff and tights (*Harry Potter*: 124), and although the ruff was worn by both men and women, the wearing of tights together with a ruff is likely to indicate a man, but the decision made by the translator as to the ghost's sex is unclear (the use of *kimi* itself makes interpretation in the Japanese as a man much more probable, but relying on this as evidence would be circular). The use of *kimi* in the riddle written by Professor Snape might also be motivated by the gender of its author, even though the note is written as if it is a collection of potions that are speaking; this may be something of a stretch, however, like understanding all characters in *Matsuoka's Harry Potter* as using speech characteristic of women because the translator is a woman. Certainly, there doesn't appear to be anything explicit in the riddle in the source text to indicate that the speaker (whether that be Professor Snape or the assortment of potions) is male. Regardless of the position one takes as to the unnamed ghost and the riddle, the sorting hat is certainly not characterised as male or female in the source text.[1]

There are also no clear examples of a speaker addressing a social superior as *kimi* in any of the corpora, with the possible exception of a single instance in *Matsuoka's Harry Potter*: Professor Quirrell addresses Professor Snape with this pronoun once. Professor Quirrell and Professor Snape are both faculty members at Hogwarts, but at the time of the conversation Professor Quirrell appears to be afraid of Professor Snape, suggesting *de facto* inferiority.

Tables 2.8 to 2.10 provide an overview of who uses *anata* to whom in the corpora. For the purposes of this overview, variations such as *anta* or *anata-sama* have not been subsumed within the category of *anata*, so as to avoid

Table 2.8 Speaker and addressee where *anata* is used in *Matsuoka's Harry Potter*

Speaker	Addressee
Vernon Dursley	Petunia Dursley (wife)
Unnamed wizard on the street	Vernon Dursley
Petunia Dursley	Vernon Dursley (husband)
Professor Dumbledore	Professor McGonagall
Professor McGonagall	Professor Dumbledore Harry Potter Draco Malfoy Neville Longbottom Hermione Granger
Harry Potter	Hagrid Dedalus Diggle Professor Quirrell Firenze (centaur)
Unnamed wizard at the Leaky Cauldron pub	Harry Potter
Draco Malfoy	Parvati Patil
Ollivander	Harry Potter
Mrs. Weasley	Ginny Weasley (daughter) Fred Weasley (son) George Weasley[P] (son)
Hermione Granger	Hagrid Harry Potter Ron Weasley

(continued)

Table 2.8 Cont.

Speaker	Addressee
Professor Snape	Professor Quirrell
Professor Filch	Harry Potter's class[P]
The Mirror of Erised	Anyone who views the mirror (the pronoun is written in reverse たなあ)
Bane (centaur)	Hagrid
Firenze (centaur)	Bane (centaur)
Madam Pomfrey	Harry Potter

Table 2.9 Speaker and addressee where *anata* is used in *Yamamoto's The Hobbit*

Speaker	Addressee
The narrator	The reader(s)
Bilbo Baggins	Gandalf
	Dwalin
	Kili
	Thorin
	The elf-king
	Bard
Gandalf	The dwarves (reported by Dori)
	The elf-king
Dwalin	Bilbo Baggins
Balin	Bilbo Baggins
The dwarves	Bilbo Baggins
	Gandalf
Kili	Bilbo Baggins
Thorin	Gandalf
	The great goblin
	Beorn
Gloin	Bilbo Baggins
Elrond	The dwarves and Gandalf[P]
Dori	Gandalf
Nori	Beorn
Ori	Beorn
Bard	Bilbo Baggins

any risk of blurring the lines on the propriety of usage. To give an example of the importance of such distinctions, in *Yamamoto's The Hobbit*, Thorin addresses Gandalf (high status but somewhat more familiar) and Bilbo (lower status but not yet familiar) as *anta*, but Beorn (seemingly high status and not familiar) and the great goblin (high status and hostile) as *anata*; collapsing these variations into a single item would lose distinctions that appear to be significant.

Table 2.10 Speaker and addressee where *anata* is used in *Seta's The Hobbit*

Speaker	Addressee
Bilbo Baggins	Gandalf
	Fili[P]
	Kili[P]
	Thorin
	Beorn
	The elf-king
	Forest elves[P]
	Smaug (dragon)
	Bard
Gandalf	Thorin
	Lord of the eagles
	Beorn
	Dain
Balin	Bilbo Baggins
Thorin and company	Bilbo Baggins (in a note)
The dwarves	Gandalf
Thorin	Bilbo Baggins
	The great goblin
	The lake-men
Gloin	Bilbo Baggins
Elrond	Bilbo Baggins
	Thorin
Dori	Bilbo Baggins
Beorn	Thorin
The elf-king	Bilbo Baggins
	Gandalf
Forest elves	Bilbo Baggins
Master of Lake-town	Thorin
Roäc (a thrush)	Thorin[P]
	Balin[P]
	Bard
Lake-men	Bilbo Baggins
	Other lake-men
Bard	Bilbo Baggins
	Thorin
	Master of Lake-town
Dain's company	Bard and the army from Lake-town[P]

Even just a cursory comparison at the usage of *anata* (Tables 2.8 to 2.10) to that of *kimi* (Tables 2.5 to 2.7) suggests the following differences with respect to distribution in the corpora. First, *anata* does indeed appear to be more available to female speakers than *kimi*, as indicated by the increase in female speakers appearing in Table 2.8 as opposed to Table 2.5. Second, there does appear to be a preference for speakers who use both *kimi* and *anata* to use the *kimi* for addressees of lower status than *anata*. In *Yamamoto's The Hobbit*, for example, Thorin uses *kimi* to address Bilbo Baggins and the dwarves in his own service, but *anata* to address Gandalf, the great goblin, and Beorn. It is also interesting to note that in certain instances the asymmetry between speakers is crystalised very clearly in the second-person pronouns they use to address one another: in *Matsuoka's Harry Potter*, for instance, Bane addresses his fellow centaur Firenze as *kimi*, where Firenze uses *anata* for Bane. Although Bane's conception of himself as socially superior comes across in the source text through his blunt criticism of Firenze's behaviour, this distillation of their perception of the relationship in the Japanese is something of a novelty.

Let us now turn to *omae*, in Tables 2.11 to 2.13. For the purposes of these tables, instances of *omae* as both お前 and おまえ have been subsumed into a single category. Some speakers also use the variant *omae-san* (the addition of the honorific suffix *san* to the pronoun *omae*). Because the number of speaker-addressee pair for which *omae-san* appears is relatively rare in the corpora, the decision was taken to include these in the tables, clearly marked as such by a bracketed reference to *omae-san*. Please note, in particular, the references to "also *omae-san* singular" in Table 2.11, for Hagrid addressing Ron Weasley and Hermione Granger in *Matsuoka's Harry Potter*; Hagrid uses plural forms of *omae* to address groups including both of these addressees, but never

Table 2.11 Speaker and addressee where *omae* is used in *Matsuoka's Harry Potter*

Speaker	Addressee
Vernon Dursley	Dudley Dursley (son)
	Petunia Dursley (wife)
	Harry Potter (nephew)
Petunia Dursley	Dudley Dursley (son)
	Harry Potter (nephew)
Hagrid	Vernon Dursley
	Harry Potter
	Draco Malfoy
	Neville Longbottom
	Ron Weasley[P]
	(also *omae-san* singular)
	Hermione Granger[P]
	(also *omae-san* singular)
	Professor Filch
	Norbert (pet dragon)
	Ronan (*omae-san*)
Professor Quirrell	Harry Potter
Draco Malfoy	Crabbe[P]
	Goyle[P]
Ollivander	Hagrid (*omae-san*)
George Weasley	Ron Weasley
Ron Weasley	Draco Malfoy
Voldemort	Harry Potter

Table 2.12 Speaker and addressee where *omae* is used in *Yamamoto's The Hobbit*

Speaker	Addressee
Bilbo Baggins	Bilbo Baggins (himself)
	Sting (speaker's sword)
	Smaug (dragon)
	Roäc (a thrush)
	Dwarves[P]
	Gollum
Gandalf	Trolls[P]
	Dain
Dwarves	Bilbo Baggins
Thorin	Bilbo Baggins
	Bard
Beorn	Bilbo Baggins[P]
	Gandalf[P]
The elf-king	Balin and the dwarves[P]
	Thorin and the dwarves[P]
Forest elves	Bilbo Baggins
Smaug (dragon)	Bilbo Baggins
Roäc (a thrush)	Bard
Bard	Bilbo Baggins
	Bard's arrow
Dain's company	Bard and the army from Lake-town[P]

Table 2.13 Speaker and addressee where *omae* is used in *Seta's The Hobbit*

Speaker	Addressee
Bilbo Baggins	Bilbo Baggins (himself)
	Gandalf (*omae-san*)
	Sting (speaker's sword)
Gandalf	Bilbo Baggins
Thorin	Bombur
Eagle	Another eagle
Beorn	Thorin and the dwarves
Nori	Dori
Forest elves	Bilbo Baggins
Smaug (dragon)	Bilbo Baggins
Bard	Bard's arrow

addresses either in the singular as simply *omae* (without the suffix *-san*). This distinction would appear to be important because where plural forms of *omae* are used, it is likely that Harry Potter (whom Hagrid does address as simply *omae*) is the principal of the group.

It would appear that there are no clear examples in the corpora that defy the expectation that *omae* not be used to address a superior. We must be careful, however, to note that in some cases this conclusion might appear to rest on circular logic. For example, we see from Table 2.12 that in *Yamamoto's The Hobbit*, the elf-king uses *omae* to refer to Thorin and his company of dwarves. It is difficult to be certain in any objective sense of whether the elf-king would consider Thorin (a putative king-in-exile of his people) a social inferior, equal, or superior. Thus, to take the use of *omae* as evidence of the elf-king's perception of himself as at least Thorin's equal, and then to rely on that as evidence that *omae* is only used to address equal's or inferiors, creates something of a trap. However, in the instances that the elf-king uses *omae* to address Thorin, Thorin is his prisoner, and the narrator explicitly states that the elves were treating the Thorin "not too gently, for they did not love dwarves, and thought he was an enemy" (*The Hobbit*: 189).

It is also interesting to observe that *omae* is the second-person pronoun of choice for addressing inanimate objects in one's possession. It is *omae* that Bilbo Baggins uses to address his sword Sting, and that Bard uses to address the black arrow with which he slays the dragon Smaug, in both *Yamamoto's The Hobbit* and *Seta's The Hobbit*. Bilbo Baggins also uses this pronoun to address himself in both of these texts, further suggesting that *omae* is appropriate for addressees that are extremely clearly identified as within one's in-group (it is difficult to imagine closer membership of an in-group than the speaker themselves or their property).

Only one female speaker is observed as using *omae* in *Matsuoka's Harry Potter*. This is Petunia Dursley, who uses the term to address her nephew Harry Potter and her son Dudley Dursley. Although Martin (1975/2004: 1079) notes that "[t]he pronoun omae (plural omaé-táti) 'you' is deprecatory except when used to children or younger relatives within the family," the reader of *Matsuoka's Harry Potter* might pick up on the difference between the two mothers seen addressing their children: Petunia Dursley uses *omae* where Mrs Weasley uses *anata* for her children Ginny, Fred, and George Weasley. Most readers of the source text would agree with an identification of Mrs Weasley as an archetypically caring and warm-hearted mother; although Petunia Dursley is portrayed as devoted to her son Dudley, she is also revealed as capable of extreme coldness (towards Harry Potter himself in particular). It also cannot be discounted that the interactions between Mrs Weasley and her children take place in a public setting, while the reader is exposed to conversations between Petunia Dursley and Dudley Dursley and Harry Potter in the privacy of their home. The presence of other listeners, or the potential of being overheard, may have a bearing on the choice of second-person pronouns.

2.5.2 Rare Pronouns and Distinctive Voices

Both translations of *The Hobbit* show the creative use of second-person pronoun choice as a way of distinguishing certain characters or category of character. In *Yamamoto's The Hobbit*, for example, the very rough *temē* is only used by the three trolls and, apart from its use in a single song, the pronoun *nanji* is only used by the thrush Roäc. *Seta's The Hobbit* similarly only sees *temē* used by the three trolls, and *onushi* by giant spiders. These pronoun choices allow the translators to immediately endow characters with distinctive voices, in a way not present in the source text.

2.6 Pronoun Alternation

In the previous section it was shown that there were some general themes in terms of the second-person pronouns used by certain speakers to certain addressees. However, it was also acknowledged that these distributions were not rigid. In other words, simply knowing some basic facts about the sex, age, and social status of the speaker and addressee is not in itself enough to predict the second-person pronoun used. This is suggested by the fact that the pronoun selection is not identical in *Yamamoto's The Hobbit* and *Seta's The Hobbit*, but there is always the possibility that such differences are explicable by differences in the translators' perceptions of the relationships in the source text, idiolect of the translator, or even language changes in the time between the two translations.

Such potential explanations, however, would not explain the phenomenon of the second-person pronoun used by a given speaker to a given addressee changing within a single text. In this section we will take a look at some examples of such variation from the corpora. This can happen over the course of a narrative, but also within a single conversation, and occasionally even within a single utterance. These switches from one second-person pronoun to another can help to shed light on factors other than social standing that play a role in pronoun selection, as the relative social standing of the speaker and addressee are often unchanged.

2.6.1 Alternation across the Narrative

There are far too many speaker–addressee pairs in the corpora for us to look in any detail at shifts in second-person pronoun use across all of them. We will instead look at one of the key relationships from within the corpora, and one that allows comparison across two of them: that of Bilbo Baggins and Thorin Oakenshield in *The Hobbit*. Table 2.14 shows the full range of address terms used by Thorin to Bilbo in *Yamamoto's The Hobbit*.[2]

Table 2.14 is, of course, a rather blunt instrument. Although the higher frequency of the address terms *kimi* and *Baggins-kun* does suggest a probability that Thorin settles into a position of perceived superiority or at least equality with Bilbo, it really is necessary to observe the places in the narrative in which the address terms are used to be sure, especially when one bears in mind the fact that second-person references are also often omitted (second-person pronouns or other address terms are omitted with respect to thirty occurrences in the source text, versus overt inclusion in thirty-eight instances).

Table 2.14 Address terms used by Thorin Oakenshield to Bilbo Baggins in *Yamamoto's The Hobbit*

Japanese as it appears in the text	Transliteration	Notes[6]	Frequency
バギンズどの	Baggins-dono	The surname Baggins, with the honorific suffix *dono*.	1
あんた	anta		2
ビルボ殿	Bilbo-dono	The given name Bilbo, with the honorific suffix *dono*. This is used on a note left by Thorin and company to Bilbo.	2
貴殿	Kiden	This is used on a note left by Thorin and company to Bilbo.	1
二人とも	futaritomo	Thorin is addressing Bilbo Baggins and Balin, a dwarf of Thorin's company.	1
君	kimi		9
バギンズ君	Baggins-kun	The surname Baggins, with the suffix *kun*.	6
お前 (once as おまえ)	omae		7
この、ろくでなし のホビットめ。	kono, roku de nashi no hobbit-me	For "You miserable hobbit!" in the source text.	1
この、寸足らず の…押入め!	kono, suntarazu no… oshiire-me!	For "You undersized-burglar!" in the source text.	1
みんな	minna	Thorin is addressing Bilbo Baggins, Gandalf, and possibly any and all of the Lake-men and elves gathered to besiege him.	1
ドブネズミの曽孫 め、	dobunezumi no himago-me,	For "you descendant of rats" in the source text.	1
善良な泥棒くん、	zenryō-na dorobō-kun	For "good thief" in the source text.	1
自分	jibun	The reflexive pronoun *jibun*.	1
暖かな＜西＞の子 よ、	atataka-na "nishi" no ko yo	For "child of the kindly West" in the source text.	1

Observing the second-person references in context, however, does indeed reveal that their use appears to track closely with the changing relationship between Thorin and Bilbo. The more respectful *Baggins-dono* and *anta* are used when Thorin first meets Bilbo as a guest in Bilbo's house. As has been mentioned earlier in this chapter, Thorin's use of *anta* for Bilbo contrasts with his use of *anata* for Gandalf, Beorn, and the great goblin; Thorin appears to consider this latter group as closer to being his equals.

There is then a brief interlude in the form of a note left by "Thorin & Co.," in which the language is more formal and respectful (including the somewhat archaic and highly deferential *kiden*, the only instance of Thorin addressing Bilbo in this way), after which *kimi* and *Baggins-kun* become dominant. By this point, Bilbo has entered into Thorin's service (as a professional burglar), and so this change in address term does reflect a change in the relative status of the two parties. Where, in the source text, Thorin addresses Bilbo as *Mr Baggins* and *you* at both their first meeting and after Bilbo has entered his service, in *Yamamoto's The Hobbit* the way that these terms are translated changes to suit the relationship of the speaker and addressee.

The appearances of *omae*, and the three offensive references ("You miserable hobbit!," "You undersized-burglar!," and "you descendant of rats") all appear in the same brief conversation, when Thorin sees that Bilbo has abandoned his company to take a priceless treasure to Thorin's enemies, so that it can be used to bargain for a share of the gold that Thorin and his company have reclaimed. The shift to a more direct pronoun (not to mention the name-calling), reflect this new position of hostility. While the insults appear in the source text, and are more-or-less closely translated in the Japanese, we once again see the simple English second-person pronoun *you* represented by a range of Japanese equivalents – Yamamoto's Thorin has used *anta*, *kimi*, and *omae* as second-person pronouns when speaking to a single counterpart.

Table 2.15 Address terms used by Bilbo Baggins to Thorin Oakenshield in *Yamamoto's The Hobbit*

Japanese as it appears in the text	Transliteration	Notes	Frequency
トリン・オウクンシ ルド	*Thorin Oakenshield*		1
あなた	*anata*		3
あなたがた	*anatakata*	This is a plural form, including Thorin's company of dwarves in the group of reference.	1
おお、トラインの息 子なるトリン・オウ クンシルドさん	*ō, Thrain no musuko naru Thorin Oakenshield-san*	For "O Thorin Thrain's son Oakenshield" in the source text.	1
トリン	*Thorin*		2
トリンさん	*Thorin-san*		2
＜山の王＞よ	*'yama no ō' yo*	For "King under the Mountain" in the source text.	1

Looking at the address terms used by Bilbo for Thorin in the same translation reveals the asymmetry in second-person reference (see Table 2.15). Not only does Bilbo overtly refer to Thorin far less frequently, but when he does, he uses a name or *anata*. It should be noted also that of the six occasions that Bilbo addresses Thorin by name in *Yamamoto's The Hobbit*, two are in situations where Bilbo is running around in a panic looking for his companions and calling their names (トリン・オウクンシルド and one instance of トリン！). Another three appear within rebukes (even if one is a somewhat gentle rebuke, calling Thorin, seemingly enchanted by the retrieval of his ancestral treasure, back to his senses to help formulate a plan of defence against the dragon Smaug).

(26)
[Bilbo Baggins to Thorin, upon rescuing the latter from imprisonment by the forest elves but treated impolitely by the latter due to the uncomfortable manner of escape]
Well, are you alive or are you dead?

(The Hobbit: 216)

ちょっとお聞きますが、トリンさん、あなたとにかく死んでいないですよね

(Yamamoto's The Hobbit, vol. 2: 88)

(27)
[Bilbo Baggins to Thorin, reminding Thorin that they are in danger and need to defend themselves against the return of the dragon Smaug]
Thorin!... What next? We are armed, but what good has any armour ever been before against Smaug the Dreadful?

(The Hobbit: 268)

トリン！... おつぎはどうする？鎧は着たけど、＜恐怖の大王＞スマウグを前にして、今までよろいがどんな役にたったの？

(Yamamoto's The Hobbit, vol. 2: 167)

(28)
[Bilbo Baggins to Thorin, after Thorin has angrily and rudely criticised Bilbo for surrendering a priceless treasure to Thorin's foes]
Is this all the service of you and your family that I was promised, Thorin?

(The Hobbit: 308)

”下部としてお仕えする”というのは、そういうことだったのですか、トリンさん？

(Yamamoto's The Hobbit, vol. 2: 226)

Not only do these rebukes account for fully half of the instances of Bilbo addressing Thorin by name, but they constitute three of the four times that Bilbo uses Thorin's given name only (without the epithet/surname Oakenshield). There are no examples of Bilbo addressing Thorin by given name only outside of these exceptional cases of panic (where Bilbo is just shouting names in lists, rather than using these names in any kind of grammatical position like subject or object, meaning that there is no question of attributing an event to the person here) or rebuke, where the speaker is less likely to be concerned about taking a more deferential tone. It is also interesting that one of only three times that Bilbo uses *anata* to refer to Thorin is also contained within one of these rebukes. The instance where *anatakata* is used also appears within a rebuke:

(29)
[Bilbo Baggins to Thorin, continuing from example 26]
Are you still in prison, or are you free? If you want food, and if you want to go on with this silly adventure – it's yours after all and not mine – you had better slap your arms and rub your legs and try and help me get the others out while there is a chance!

(*The Hobbit*: 216)

それに、ここはもう地獄じゃないですよねえ？もしも何か食べたいのなら、もしもこのくだらない冒険をまだ続けたいという気がおありなら—ボク自身のためじゃなくって、<u>あなたかた</u>のためにこんなことやってるんですよ！—さっさと腕や足を揉むなり、さするなりして、ボクに手をかしてくださいよ。チャンスがあるうちに他の連中を出さなきゃ！

(*Yamamoto's The Hobbit*, vol. 2: 89)

In fact, example 29 shows the only instance where Bilbo uses a second-person pronoun in the position of a subject with respect to Thorin. The other uses are marked with genitive particles or the comitative particle (the example of *anatakata* is already captured in example 29).

(30)
[Bilbo Baggins to Thorin]
I am sure it reflects great credit on your grandfather, but you cannot pretend that you ever made the vast extent of his wealth clear to me.

(*The Hobbit*: 246)

<u>あなたの</u>お祖父さんがすごい人だったことはわかるけど、でも、そんなこと、ボクにはっきりと教えてくれなかったじゃないか。

(*Yamamoto's The Hobbit*, vol. 2: 134–5)

(31)
[Bilbo Baggins to Thorin]
Yet I am glad that I have shared in your perils – that has been more than any Baggins deserves.

(The Hobbit: 322)

でも、<u>あなたと</u>危難を共にできて、ボクはしあわせでした。バギンズの人間みたいな凡人にとっては、望外の好運でした

(Yamamoto's The Hobbit, vol. 2: 246)

It is more common for overt references to the second person to be omitted in Bilbo's speech to Thorin, as can be seen even in these examples (and example 29 in particular), where the second person is often an implicit argument, retrievable from the context. It must be noted that there are many more examples of Bilbo addressing the company of dwarves more generally as *kimitachi*, and these have not been included in the discussion here of address terms used by Bilbo for Thorin. This is because, in the only clear example we have that Bilbo is definitively addressing the group of dwarves with Thorin as its principal (example 29), Yamamoto has decided that Bilbo use *anatakata*. Accordingly, it is probable that in the instances in which *kimitachi* is used that Yamamoto has understood Bilbo as not addressing the group via Thorin (even if the reader may consider Thorin to be part of that group).

The discussion of the Bilbo–Thorin relationship up to this point is illustrative of how the translator has had to overtly show his interpretation of the relationships between characters in the narrative, as well as the particular context of a dialogue (e.g., instances of rebuke) in the form of second-person reference used. Although the interpretations made are likely to agree with many readers of the source text, that is not guaranteed. While the source text portrays Thorin as the exiled heir to a kingdom, and Bilbo as a more regular fellow, the source text allows a reading of Bilbo as a rather plucky individual, holding his own even in his initial meeting with Thorin – even outright challenging the dwarves as having come to his house mistakenly and having "funny faces" *(The Hobbit*: 22). Whatever the reader's interpretation of the relationship in the source text, the presentation in the target text inevitably narrows (or, at the very least, shifts) the range of interpretation available to target-text readers. This is because the use of address terms in Japanese reveals something of the relationship between interlocutors. It is extremely difficult, and maybe impossible, for the translator to remain agnostic as to these relationships while still writing an acceptable target text. The upshot of this is that readers of the target text are presented with more information about these relationships overtly.

Let us now see if the situation is similar in *Seta's The Hobbit*. Tables 2.16 and 2.17 show the second-person references used by Thorin and Bilbo to one

Table 2.16 Address terms used by Thorin Oakenshield to Bilbo Baggins in *Seta's*
The Hobbit

Japanese as it appears in the text	Transliteration	Notes	Frequency
バギンズどの	Baggins-dono		7
自分	jibun	The reflexive pronoun *jibun*.	1
あんた	anta		9
そこのふたり	soko no futari	Thorin is addressing Bilbo Baggins and Balin, a dwarf of Thorin's company.	
そちら	sochira		1
きさま	kisama		6
このみっともないホビットめ！	Kono mitto mo nai Hobbit-me!	For "You miserable hobbit!" in the source text.	1
この、いじけきったちびの——どろぼうめ！	kono, ijikekitta chibi no — dorobō-me!	For "You undersized-burglar!" in the source text.	1
みんな	minna	Thorin is addressing Bilbo Baggins, Gandalf, and possibly any and all of the Lake-men and elves gathered to besiege him.	1
このネズミのすえめ！	kono nezumi no sue-me!	For "you descendant of rats" in the source text.	1
わがしたしき忍びの者よ	Waga shitashiki shinobi no mono yo	For "good thief" in the source text.	1
あなた	anata		3
やさしい西のくにのけなげな子よ	yasashī nishi no kuni no kenage na ko yo	For "child of the kindly West" in the source text.	1

another. For the purposes of comparability to *Yamamoto's The Hobbit*, we examine only references to Thorin in the singular, or where Thorin is definitively the principal of a plural reference (a single occurrence where this is the only available interpretation because Thorin is the only addressee present, and two occasions where other content in the discourse makes it clear that Bilbo is speaking directly to Thorin). It is necessary to omit most references to the dwarves as a group in the second person in *Seta's The Hobbit* because, unlike *Yamamoto's The Hobbit*, Bilbo continues to use a plural form of the same second-person pronoun he uses for Thorin as an individual when addressing the dwarves as a group. This makes it uncertain whether Bilbo is using the

Table 2.17 Address terms used by Bilbo Baggins to Thorin Oakenshield in *Seta's The Hobbit*

Japanese as it appears in the text	Transliteration	Notes	Frequency
トーリン・オーケンシールドやーい	Thorin Oakenshield yāi		1
あんた	anta		1
あんたがた	antagata	A plural address, where Thorin is the only addressee present.	1
あなた	anata		1
自分	Jibun		1
おお、スラインのむすこトーリン・オーケンシールドどの	ō, Thrain no musuko Thorin Oakenshield-dono	For "O Thorin Thrain's son Oakenshield" in the source text.	1
あんたがた	antagata		2
トーリン	Thorin		3
山の下のまことの王よ	yama no shita no makoto no ō yo	For "King under the Mountain" in the source text.	1
トーリン・オーケンシールドよ	Thorin Oakenshield yo		1

same pronoun because he is addressing the group through Thorin as principal or for another reason.

Seta's The Hobbit also has an asymmetry between Thorin, who more generally uses *anta* for Bilbo, and Bilbo, who only uses a second-person pronoun to address Thorin during rebukes. Instances of the overt address terms listed in Table 2.17 that occur within rebukes are shown in the following examples.

(32)

[Bilbo Baggins to Thorin, upon rescuing the latter from imprisonment by the forest elves but treated impolitely by the latter due to the uncomfortable manner of escape]

Are you still in prison, or are you free? If you want food, and if you want to go on with this silly adventure – it's yours after all and not mine – you had better slap your arms and rub your legs and try and help me get the others out while there is a chance!

(*The Hobbit*: 216)

いったい<u>あんた</u>は、まだ牢屋にとじこめられているんですか、自由になったんですか、どっちです？もしごはんが食べたければ、いや、このばかばかしい冒険をつづけたければ（だいたい、これは<u>あんたがた</u>のもので、わたしの冒険ではないじゃありませんか）腕をさすり、足をなぜて、立ちあがり、まだチャンスがあるうちに、わ

たしの手だすけをして、ほかの者たちを出した方が、いいんじゃあ
りませんか？

(Seta's The Hobbit, vol. 2: 51)

(33)
[Bilbo Baggins to Thorin, rebuking the latter for speaking as if Bilbo had
not already been of considerable service to the company when it is time
for Bilbo to perform his work as a burglar]
If you mean you think it is my job to go into the secret passage first,
O Thorin Thrain's son Oakenshield, may your beard grow ever longer…
say so at once and have done! I have got you out of two messes already,
which were hardly in the original bargain, so that I am, I think, already
owed some reward.

(The Hobbit: 237)

おお、スラインのむすこトニリン― オニケンシニルドどの、お話ちゅ
うですが、あなたはこの秘密の入口にまっさきにはいるのが、わ
たしの仕事だと考えていることをおっしゃりたいのなら、それほど
だらだらと、おひげをはやすほど話をひきのばす必要はありますま
い。わたしはこれまでに、二度の急場からあなたがたを助けだし
た。

(Seta's The Hobbit, vol. 2: 88)

(34)
[Bilbo Baggins to Thorin, reminding Thorin that they are in danger and
need to defend themselves against the return of the dragon Smaug]
Thorin!… What next? We are armed, but what good has any armour ever
been before against Smaug the Dreadful?

(The Hobbit: 268)

トニリン！…これからどうします？わたしたちはみなよろいをつけ
ました。けれども、どんなによいよろいを着こんでも、おそろしき
ものなるスマウグめに、立ちむかえるものでしょうか？

(Seta's The Hobbit, vol. 2: 142)

(35)
[Bilbo Baggins to Thorin, after Thorin has angrily and rudely criticised
Bilbo for surrendering a priceless treasure to Thorin's foes]
You may remember saying that I might choose my own fourteenth share?
… Is this all the service of you and your family that I was promised,
Thorin?

(The Hobbit: 308)

あなたは、前にわたしが、自分のわけまえを自分でえらんでよろし
いといったことをおぼえているでしょう？トニリン、あなたは、自

分の子々孫々までわたしの役にたちたいとまでいったではありませ
んか？

(*Seta's The Hobbit*, vol. 2: 211)

The only time Bilbo addresses Thorin by given name alone is on one of the
occasions that Bilbo is in a panic and calling a list of names in the party, in a
terrified attempt to locate them. The only time that Bilbo uses an overt second-
person pronoun to address Thorin outside of these rebukes is the moment of
heightened intimacy when they are reconciled on Thorin's deathbed.

(36)
[Bilbo Baggins to Thorin]
Yet I am glad that I have shared in your perils – that has been more than
any Baggins deserves.

(*The Hobbit*: 322)

でもわたしは、命をかけて<u>あなた</u>と冒険をともにしたことが、うれ
しくてなりません。

(*Seta's The Hobbit*, vol. 2: 235)

Seta's The Hobbit also resembles *Yamamoto's The Hobbit* in the translator's
choice to have a shift in the second-person pronouns Thorin uses to address
Bilbo during the conflict where Thorin discovers that Bilbo has handed a
priceless treasure to Thorin's foes. *Yamamoto's The Hobbit* had a switch from the
more usual *kimi* to *omae*, and *Seta's The Hobbit* has Thorin changing from *anta*
to the very abrasive *kisama*. Although not an identical change, the translations
both provide a move from a more respectful to a less respectful second-person
pronoun for this hostile context. Indeed, it might be relevant to note Tanaka's
(2016: 216) observation that the use of personal pronouns such as *omae* and
kisama is characteristic of rude language as used in scenes of conflict in manga.

Although the use of address terms in *Seta's The Hobbit* also portrays the
asymmetry typical of a relationship between a superior and inferior, *Seta's
The Hobbit* does not feature a transition from the second-person pronoun
from Thorin's initial meeting with Bilbo to the period after Bilbo has entered
Thorin's company. This would appear to indicate that Seta has not interpreted
this development as of as great a significance as Yamamoto, and the reader of
these translations is therefore likely to have slightly different impressions of
the relationship between these individuals during the narrative.

2.6.2 Local Alternations

Let us now examine some examples where pronoun changes occur locally.
One of the clearest examples of the difference in the pragmatic effect of
second-person pronouns comes from the translations of *The Hobbit*, where
both *Yamamoto's The Hobbit* and *Seta's The Hobbit* demonstrate a pronoun

shift in the same stretch of text. The passage in question concerns the arrival of reinforcements, led by the dwarf Dain son of Nain, who have come to relieve the siege of Thorin and his company by a combined force of elves and men. Emissaries from Dain's army approach Bard. The relevant sections of text have been underlined in the following extract from the source text, and the translations of those underlined sections of text are provided (with the second-person pronouns underlined in the Japanese).

(37)
[Messengers from Dain to Bard, and narration]
"But who are you that sit in the plain as foes before defended walls?" This, of course, in the polite and rather old-fashioned language of such occasions, meant simply: "You have no business here. We are going on, so make way or we shall fight you!"

(The Hobbit: 310–11)

しかし、城壁のまえの敵よろしく、平原に座りこむ貴殿らはどなたですか？... お前らにこんなところいてもらっては困る。われわれは先に進むぞ。だから道を開けろ。さもないと、攻撃するぞ。

(Yamamoto's The Hobbit, vol. 2: 229–30)

して、防壁を前に敵のごとくに平地に陣どるあなたがたは、いったいどなたか？... きさまらは、ここに用はない。われらのゆくてに、道をあけるか？とめだてすると、うちやぶるぞ。

(Seta's The Hobbit, vol. 2: 215)

Although the selection of pronouns is not identical in the Japanese texts, there is a clear shift in both from the actual politer speech of Dain's messengers to the narrator's explanation of what they really mean: *Yamamoto's The Hobbit* switches from *kidenra* to *omaera*, and *Seta's The Hobbit* from *anatagata* to *kisamara*. Although possibly so obvious that it goes without saying, this clearly demonstrates that regardless of a speaker's understanding of the relative social status of their addressee, that speaker always has a choice as to how polite they want to be in their speech, or whether they would rather take a more direct and hostile approach. Although the underlined sections from the source text in example 37 also demonstrate a shift from a polite to a hostile approach, this is not reflected in pronoun selection. In the Japanese, there is a change in register in both translations – this is especially distinct in *Yamamoto's The Hobbit*, where there is also a shift from the politer *desu/masu* predicate endings to the plain form, as well as a very blunt imperative *akero*, and two appearances of the rough sentence-final particle *zo* (which also appears once in the version from Seta).

There is also an example from *The Hobbit* where Bilbo Baggins, Gandalf, Thorin, and Thorin's company of dwarves have arrived uninvited at the house of Beorn, a powerful and dangerous shapeshifter. Beorn is addressing Thorin in a somewhat respectful manner, and suddenly changes the direction of the conversation (the second-person references have been underlined in the Japanese text):

(38)
[Beorn to Thorin]
I am not over fond of dwarves; but if it is true that you are Thorin (son of Thrain, son of Thror, I believe), and that your companion is respectable, and that you are enemies of goblins and are not up to any mischief in my lands – what are you up to, by the way?

(*The Hobbit*: 137)

おれは、ドワーフがとくに好きというのではないが、きらいではない。あなたがトーリンであるなら、あのスロールの息子スラインの、息子であろう。ではその連れも、しかるべきもので、みな、ゴブリンどもの目のかたきであり、おれの土地にいるあいだは、いたずらをせぬということなら―ところで、いったいおまえたち、なにをはじめたんだな？

(*Seta's The Hobbit*, vol. 1: 239)

Seta's The Hobbit has a switch from *anata* to *omaetachi* in Beorn's speech here (*Yamamoto's The Hobbit* does not have a switch in pronoun here, instead omitting a pronoun with respect to the text after the dash). It would appear that Seta has reflected the switch from the more friendly and conciliatory attitude towards Thorin (even if couched in a clear position of basic underlying hostility towards dwarves) to a more direct questioning, with a similar shift from the politer *anata* to the blunter *omaetachi*. One observes an instance of a similar rapid change in *Matsuoka's Harry* Potter, with Hagrid moving from *anta* to *omae-san* when addressing Harry Potter (the second-person pronouns have been underlined in the Japanese text).

(39)
[Hagrid to Harry Potter]
Sent owls off ter all yer parents' old school friends, askin' fer photos...
Knew yeh didn't have any... D'yeh like it?

(*Harry Potter*: 327)

あんたのご両親の学友たちにフクロウを送って、写真を集めたんだ。だっておまえさんは一枚も持っとらんし...気に入ったか？

(*Matsuoka's Harry Potter*: 468)

The quoted text is fairly self-explanatory in terms of context but, for the avoidance of any doubt, Hagrid has just presented Harry Potter with an album of photographs of Harry's parents, who died while he was a baby and of whom he previously had no photographs. It is extremely unlikely that the change in second-person pronoun selection here is motivated by a changed perception in the relative social status of the interlocutors, so why is there such a rapid change? It might be worth returning to first principles here, and the idea of a preference for less directness when it comes to pinning actions or thoughts to an individual, especially one's addressee – and that this preference becomes stronger in at least a general correlation with the perceived relative social status of the addressee.[3] Although in many cases the preference is to achieve this by omitting second-person pronouns as much as possible, certain second-person pronouns may be understood as more direct and others as less so. The perceived relative social status of the addressee will inform the decision of whether to use a pronoun and which pronoun to select if one is used, but shifting pronoun use indicates that it cannot be the only factor. In example 39, it is likely that the use of the more deferential and somewhat periphrastic *anata*[4] was used to soften the tone due to the sensitivity of the reference to the addressee's deceased parents. There is then a shift back to a more direct and intimate form *omae* when Hagrid turns the discussion back to Harry himself, marked as a grammatical theme by the particle *wa*. We have seen, in the discussion of rebukes earlier, how the nature of the discussion itself can influence the choice of address term.

Another shift in the choice of second-person pronoun that has dramatic consequences occurs at the dramatic climax of *Matsuoka's Harry Potter*, when the titular protagonist finally reaches the Philosopher's Stone and confronts the mystery antagonist who has beaten him to the chase. During the conversation that follows, and with apologies for the spoiler, Professor Quirrell shifts between using *kimi* (the second-person pronoun he had more generally used to address Harry previously) to *omae*. It is interesting that, although Quirrell is undoubtedly hostile towards Harry throughout this conversation, he only shifts to using *omae* when announcing that he is going to kill him. This may reflect an attempt to show that Quirrell is angrier when making such a statement, although it is also possible that the translator is deliberately trying to allow some time for the character to explain his motivation before revealing this hostility outright. The shift to the use of *omae* also serves to foreshadow the imminent introduction of Lord Voldemort, the real nemesis throughout the series, who has been residing on the back of Professor Quirrell's head, as *omae* is the principal second-person pronoun that Lord Voldemort himself uses to address Harry.

2.7 Conclusion

Our review of the treatment of second-person reference in the corpora appears to show that, in general, the translators have adopted a strategy of movement towards acceptable Japanese target texts – the translators have clearly all given some attention to the selection of address terms that fall within a range of acceptable target-language options (bearing in mind the widened scope provided by the fantastical or unusual nature of many characters in *Harry Potter* and *The Hobbit*). This is visible in the wide range of second-person pronouns and other address terms used within the texts, in the shift of second-person reference between the same individuals on the basis of particular contextual factors or social developments, and in the wide omission of second-person pronouns (including the adoption of alternatives such as quantity nominals). The translators have not prioritised a reflection of the source language convention by, for example, adopting a single second-person pronoun to translate all instances where *you* is used in the source text. Nevertheless, second-person pronouns appear to be more widely used for overt second-person reference in the corpora than would be expected in natural untranslated Japanese. Another way of looking at this is to differentiate between the sentential and textual level. At the sentential level the translators' choices appear to tend towards natural Japanese for the most part (with some notable exceptions, such as children addressing Hagrid by his surname only in *Matsuoka's Harry Potter*, and the creative use of rarer pronouns by particular characters or groups of characters in the translations of *The Hobbit*); at the textual level, the wider distribution of second-person pronouns seems to show some kind of traction exerted on the translators by the conventions of the source texts.

There are entire areas that we have been unable to analyse for the purposes of this publication, such as variations in orthography of second-person pronouns in the target texts (with variations observed in the orthography of *kimi* and *omae*, for example), and some of the topics we have covered would certainly bear further investigation. Even so, it is hoped that this chapter has helped to demonstrate the increased complexity in the treatment of second-person reference in Japanese when compared to English, and that translating from English to Japanese can involve (if one is to create a source text approaching acceptable Japanese) the overt expression of the translator's interpretation of pragmatic factors such as inter-character relationships.

Notes

1 It must be noted that, unfortunately, *The Hobbit* does not provide any female characters to provide data in respect of this question.
2 Please note that for the transliterations from Japanese in the tables here, where a Japanese word is itself a transliteration from the English source text, the original English word has been inserted, rather than back-transliterating (e.g., *Baggins* and *Thorin* have been given rather than *Bagginzu* or *Tōrin*).
3 Shibatani (1990/2005: 364) writes that "[f]undamental to the honorific mechanism is avoidance of direct attribution of an event to a person," but the term *event* should not be narrowly construed. As will be discussed, the preference to avoid overt attribution to a person seems to be especially strong with respect to predicates relating to thought, for example.
4 *Anata* is derived from the distal *a* deictic form and *nata*, itself derived from *no kata*, and so can loosely be understood as fundamentally coming from a reference to a direction or alternative proximal to neither the speaker nor interlocutor. Martin

(1975/2004: 1067) explains that this distal form was "chosen out of exaggerated deference."

5 The information provided in Table 2.1 and Table 2.2 does not always reflect the full entry in this dictionary; in particular, where a word has several definitions, only information related to its pronominal use has been represented here. Square brackets are used to set apart notes that are not derived from the dictionary.

6 The notes provided in Tables 2.14 to 2.17 provide additional information relating to use in the text. Where an outline has already been provided with respect to a particular pronoun, for example, such information is not reproduced here.

3 Address Terms in the Korean Translations of *The Hobbit, or There and Back Again* and *Harry Potter and the Philosopher's Stone*

This chapter performs a similar analysis to that of Chapter 2, but with respect to the Korean translations of J.K. Rowling's (1997/2014) *Harry Potter and the Philosopher's Stone* (henceforth, *Harry Potter*) and J.R.R. Tolkien's (1937/2011) *The Hobbit, or There and Back Again* (henceforth, *The Hobbit*). It will be seen that similar issues concerning differing levels of complexity in address terms pertain to this language pair.

3.1 *The Hobbit*

Let us first look at the translation of the second-person pronoun *you*, and the treatment of address terms, in Lee Mi'ae's (이미애) Korean translation (2002/2007) of *The Hobbit* (this translation will be cited as *Lee's The Hobbit* in the text that follows, to differentiate it from the source text).

3.1.1 Translation as an "In-between" Space

The linguistic space between the Korean and English languages is vast and can sometimes stretch into an irreconcilable disparity when a literary text is rendered from one language to the other. The translation of *The Hobbit* can, at times, demonstrate such limitations in translation across this language pair.

For example, when Balin meets Bilbo for the first time, he greets Bilbo by saying: "Balin at your service!" (*The Hobbit*: 10). The relationship described in this interaction is one of mutual respect, or at the very least reciprocal politeness, expressed through the humility of both characters towards one another. In the translation, "at your service" is delivered as "당신께 봉사하겠습니다" (*Lee's The Hobbit*: 27), where the honorifics of the second-person pronoun *dangsin* (당신) and the verb ending *-imnida* (입니다) indicate the modest, respectful nature of the statement. Although the latter is a form used when addressing someone of a higher (or often, distant) status and hence matches the pronoun *dangsin*, which *can* be used by someone of a higher hierarchical status, ultimately the sentence ends up sounding unnatural to native ears. This is a curious phenomenon whereby the translation sounds out-of-place, despite agreement of the honorifics in the hierarchical system,

DOI: 10.4324/9781003217466-3

as reflected in the predicate ending and the pronoun selection. Such unnaturalness could be the result of the pronoun *dangsin*'s ambiguous status in the Korean language, where it can allow both a formal and informal interpretation, depending on the situation in which it is used. Because of such ambiguity, the pronoun itself is rarely used in a verbal context, and when it is, it is often to belittle or confront the hearer (e.g., 당신이 뭔데, "how dare you") or in archaic settings in which a wife addresses her husband. The pronoun *dangsin* as a neutral second-person pronoun is a phenomenon that has come to exist only in the space of translation; the use of this word in such a manner ultimately undermines the broad scope of its possible definition and its limited use in a real conversational setting.

Another instance of such unnaturalness occurs when Thorin asks for further assistance from the bird Roäc. The source text (*The Hobbit*: 289) has "if you would earn our thanks still more, bring us news of any that draw near," which is translated as "그대가 가까이 다가온 자들의 소식을 우리에게 전해 준다면 더 고맙겠소" (*Lee's The Hobbit*: [126]). Once again, the neutral status of the second-person pronoun in English has been charged with certain hierarchical implications when rendered into Korean, as it is transformed into the archaic pronoun *geudae* (그대). *Geudae* is even less frequently used than its counterpart *dangsin*, which again reminds the native Korean readers that the translational convention expressed in *The Hobbit* is one that we cannot observe in our real lived environment – in our ordinary everyday conversations. Although this unnaturalness may perhaps be tolerated to an extent due to the fantastical, extraordinary nature of the narrative itself, what is noteworthy here is the complete invention of an unnatural pragmatic system when the narrative is brought from English to Korean. What started out as a neutral, equal relation between the characters, signified by the neutral nature of the pronoun *you*, is transformed into a variety of context-based Korean counterparts, which all immediately establish overt hierarchical relationships between the characters.

Such archaic pronouns only find modern use in this moment of translation, where establishing a hierarchy between the characters based on their intimacy, age, and social position is necessary in the cultural context. Though it is strange to use the pronoun *dangsin* in real-life conversations, this somewhat volatile word is perfectly acceptable in translation as a neutral second-person pronoun. This may not sound too natural, but in a translational space where the translator needs to take decisions to establish context, the unnaturalness becomes a product of the inevitable, often irreconcilable conflict between languages. What happens in the moment of translation is the creation of a new language – a "trans-lect," which is essentially a mediating space between languages. The addition that happens during translation under the translator's creative control of the narrative – the context, hierarchical relation, and eventually, the unnaturalness – becomes the underlying structure of a new linguistic dimension that only comes into being through translation. What is at stake during the act of translation is, then, the inevitable formation of the "trans-lect," along with the visible disparity between the languages – yet this is a discussion and negotiation that will continue at every juncture of the practice.

3.1.2 The Use of Pronouns

Korean, like Japanese, does not possess a clearly defined, closed set of personal pronouns. Consequently, a person or persons can be referred to in a diverse number of ways; pronoun choice reflects the semantic and pragmatic properties that are dependent on sociological and psychological factors, as well as gender (Suzuki 1976). Personal pronouns – in particular of the first and second persons – "are simply too loaded with semantic and pragmatic information to be generalised or used impersonally" (Kitagawa and Lehrer 1990: 756). In this way, they cannot be separated from the context in which one is speaking. A seemingly straightforward and factual sentence like "it is raining" in English cannot be completed in Korean without the speaker revealing perceptions of his/her relationship vis-à-vis the listener(s) (Kiaer, 2017). The most frequently used speech styles are: (1) the formal honorific style (*-mnida* ㅂ니다); (2) the polite style (*-yo* 요.); (3) the "half-talk" or intimate style (*banmal* 반말) (Kiaer, Guest & Li 2019).

The speaker's relationship with the listener(s) and the nature of conversation (e.g., public and private) are crucial to choosing the appropriate speech style. Relationship factors refer to the social positioning of the speaker in relation to the listener(s), such as one's occupation, age, and familial ties in comparison with the listener(s) (Byon 2017). Conversational factors are generally concerned with whether the nature of talk with the listener(s) takes place in a private or informal setting, or in a public, more formal setting. This is even tricker when pronouns enter the picture. It is particularly difficult to use second-person pronouns in Korean without first ascertaining the listener(s)'s social position in relation to oneself. If one's guess is wrong, the result may be the insulting use of an erroneous second-person pronoun. This could have devastating consequences on interpersonal relationships. Therefore, Koreans often just omit second-person pronouns and instead use address or reference terms, like kinship terms (Song 2005, Cho et al. 2019). Table 3.1 provides a list of Korean pronouns and an explanation of their usage.

As Table 3.1 demonstrates, it is very tricky to know which pronouns to use on which occasions. This poses particular problems for non-native speakers. It also poses great difficulty for online translators. Figure 3.1 is a screenshot of Google Translate's efforts at translating nine simple English utterances into Korean, and one can observe examples of mismatched pronouns and speech styles. There is no consistent pattern in the combinations of pronouns and speech styles. For example, if we look at the first-person pronoun, (1) has an explicit first-person pronoun in Korean, whereas (2) and (3) omit the first-person pronoun. As for second-person pronouns, both *dangsin* and *neo* are outputted, but their use appears to be arbitrary. The selection of sentence endings also seems to be random. Ultimately, this random selection of pronouns and sentence endings is likely to result in unnatural translations due to the high probability of pragmatic conflict (Kiaer 2021). This is a huge problem in English–Korean translation.

Table 3.1 Korean pronouns and their associated uses

Pronoun	Type	Usage	Appropriate speech style
나	First-person pronoun	- 나 (*na*) is used mostly in polite or intimate half-talk - 나 (*na*) can be used when one talks to close friends and family normally in a private situation. - First-person pronoun 나 (*na*) is unnatural when one talks to their senior both in private and public situation.	Polite or intimate
저	First-person pronoun	- 저 (*jeo*) is unnatural when one talks to close friends and family normally in a private situation. - 저 (*keo*) is natural when one talks to their senior both in private and public situation.	Polite or honorific
너	Second-person pronoun	- 너(neo) is natural when one uses it to close friends and younger siblings.	Intimate
당신	Second-person pronoun	- 당신 (*dangsin*) is natural when one uses it to an unspecific, general audience. - 당신 (*dangsin*) is natural when used between a husband and a wife. - 당신 (*dangsin*) is unnatural when one uses it to address a specific listener.	Polite or intimate
No pronoun		- It is most natural for a second-person pronoun to be omitted in colloquial Korean, except some limited cases, as stated in section 3.1.2.	Polite
그	Third-person singular pronoun	- 그 (*keu*) is unnatural in colloquial Korean, but natural in written Korean	
그녀	Third-person singular pronoun	- 그녀 (*keunyeo*) is unnatural in colloquial Korean, but natural in written Korean	
그 분	Third-person singular pronoun	- 그 분 (*keu bun*) is natural in colloquial Korean when used to refer to an addressee more senior than the speaker.	Polite
그 사람	Third-person singular pronoun	- 그 사람(*keu saram*) is unnatural in colloquial Korean when used to refer to an addressee more senior than the speaker.	

Figure 3.1 Screenshot of translations from Google Translate of English utterances featuring first- and second-person pronouns into Korean

Table 3.2 Pronoun input versus pronoun output

English input	Korean output	Location
I	*Ne* 내	Example 1
I	(omitted)	Examples 2, 3
You	*Dangsin* 당신	Examples 4, 5, 7
You	*Neo* 너	Example 6
You	(omitted)	Examples 2, 3
She	*Kunyeo* 그녀	Examples 2, 3

Table 3.3 Types of sentence ending

Sentence ending style	Location
Formal honorific	Examples 5, 9
Polite	Example 2
Intimate	Example 3
Neutral	Examples 1, 4, 8

Tables 3.2 and 3.3 map out the speech styles and pronouns that Google Translate outputs in Figure 3.1.

As can be seen in Figure 3.1, the English input tells us nothing about the addressee or the situation; as such, it is difficult to provide any explanation for Google Translate's selection of different pronouns and speech styles. Even for computer algorithms, Korean pronouns and speech styles are hard to master. For the translator, pronouns and speech styles have to be carefully negotiated, as the translator's choices create so much meaning.

The discussion of pronouns and address terms in *The Hobbit* will exclude the gender aspect for the most part, as the novel does not include any female characters. Thus, the social aspect will be the focus of the analysis of pronouns in this section.

Pronouns are used frequently in the Korean translation of *The Hobbit* and are perhaps not dropped as much as they would be in regular usage of the Korean language. The translator has chosen to translate pronouns such as *you* by determining Korean equivalents based on the situational context and background of each character and the relationship they have with the addressee. Lee Mi'ae seems to have focused on translating in a similar style to the original English version as much as possible to convey the narrative, rather than adapting the dialogue into strictly "natural," vernacular Korean.

3.1.3 The Distribution of Particular Second-Person Pronouns

In *The Hobbit*, Lee Mi'ae has translated the second-person pronoun *you* into *dangsin* (당신), *ja-ne* (자네), *geudae* (그대), *neo* (너) (and their plural equivalents when addressing a group of two or more characters).

Dangsin is the most formal pronoun used in *The Hobbit* and is used by the largest variety of characters in the novel. It appears in its singular or plural form approximately 170 times. This pronoun is used as an extremely polite form of second-person pronoun and would therefore be used with *jondaetmal* (존댓말), rather than *banmal* (반말). It should be noted that the word has different connotations in vernacular usage: it can be used between couples as a respectful, slightly formal form of address; however, it can also be used to express anger and start an argument. If a wife addressed her husband as *dangsin* in a heated argument, it would not be a sign of genuine respect but rather an expression of passive aggression used to belittle and provoke the husband. In *The Hobbit*, however, it is only used in the more respectful manner. Table 3.4 sets out who uses *dangsin*, and to whom.

Table 3.4 Speaker and addressee where *dangsin* (당신) is used in *The Hobbit*, where the hierarchical dynamic is speaker < hearer

Speaker	Addressee
Gandalf	Elvenking
	Beorn
Dwarlin	Bilbo
Bilbo	Unnamed dwarf
	Gloin
	Dwalin
	Gandalf
	Group of dwarves
	Balin
	Thorin
	Smaug

(continued)

Table 3.4 Cont.

Speaker	Addressee
	Elf
	Smaug (dragon)
	Bombur
	Bard
	Unnamed man
	The Elvenking
	Group of elves
Balin	Bilbo
	Elvenking
Dori, Nori, Ori, Oin, and Gloin	Each other
Gloin	Bilbo
Thorin	Gandalf
	Bilbo
	Bard
Dori	Gandalf
The dwarves	Bilbo
Beorn	Gandalf
The dwarves	Beorn
Group of elves	Balion
Fili	The captain
The Master	Thorin
An old thrush	Bard
Bard	The master
	Thorin
	Bilbo
	Group of dwarves
Roäc	Bilbo
	Thorin
Elf	Bilbo
Elvenking	Gandalf
	Bard

Some representative examples of the use of *dangsin* (당신) are provided here. The English source text follows the corresponding Korean dialogue extracts, and relevant parts of the text are underlined in these and all following examples in the chapter.

(1)
[Balin and Bilbo after Bilbo impresses Balin by sneaking undetected into the dwarf camp]
"Balin at your service," said he.
"Your servant, Mr. Baggins," said Bilbo.

(*The Hobbit*: 106)

"발린이 <u>당신</u>께 봉사하겠습니다."
발린이 말했다. 그러자 빌보가 답했다.
"<u>당신</u>의 시중, 나 골목쟁이네야말로."

(*Lee's The Hobbit*: 144)

Here, both Balin and Bilbo are highly respectful of each other, introducing
themselves in a humble manner.

(2)
[Thorin and Dori greeting Beorn for the first time]
"Thorin Oakenshield, at your service! Dori at your service!" said the two
dwarves bowing again.
"I don't need your service, thank you," said Beorn, "but I expect you need
mine. I am not over-fond of dwarves; but if it is true you are Thorin (son
of Thrain, son of Thror, I believe), and that your companion is respectable, and that you are enemies of goblins and are not up to any mischief
in my lands – what are you up to, by the way?"

(*The Hobbit*: 137)

"참나무방패 소린<u>입니다</u>. 당신께 봉사하겠습니다! 도리도 <u>당신</u>께 봉사
하겠습니다!"
두 난쟁이가 다시 절을 하며 말했다.
"됐네, 그럴 것까진 없어. 오히려 자네들한테 내 도움이 필요할 것 같군.
나는 난쟁이들을 그다지 좋아하지 않아. 하지만 자네가 정말로 스로르
의 아들인 스라인의 아들 소린이라면, 그리고 자네 일행이 점잖고, 고블
린의 적이며, 내 땅에서 말썽을 피우지 않을 거라면...그런데 자네들은
대체 뭘 하려는 건가?"

(*Lee's The Hobbit*: 176)

Beorn is later described in the same chapter as a character who is "never very
polite" – he also speaks to Gandalf in *banmal*. However, he still refers to
Thorin and the dwarves as *dangsin*.

Ja-ne (자네) is the most frequently used second-person pronoun; a variation
of this term appears over 200 times in total in *The Hobbit*. Gandalf uses this
pronoun when addressing Bilbo and the dwarves throughout the novel. It is a
polite term used by an older individual with distinctly higher status to show
respect to a younger, lower-ranking addressee. Therefore, unlike *dangsin,* it is
used while speaking in *banmal* throughout the text. It is a rather archaic term
and is not used frequently in modern Korean language. However, it is still
used occasionally by speakers of regional dialects in areas such as *Jeolla-do*
(전라도). It is predominantly used by men rather than women; for example, a
father-in-law may refer to their son-in-law as *ja-ne*. According to Kang (2007),
ja-ne is also used by people in their forties to refer to elders, in Jeolla-do. This
is not the case in any other province. Table 3.5 sets out who uses *ja-ne* (자네)
in the translation, and to whom.

Table 3.5 Speaker and addressee where *ja-ne* (자네) is used in *The Hobbit*, where the hierarchical dynamic is speaker > hearer

Speaker	Addressee
Elvenking	Bilbo
Gandalf	Bilbo
	Thorin
	The dwarves
Elrond	Gandalf, Bilbo, and the dwarves
Balin	Bilbo
Eagle	Bilbo
Beorn	Thorin and Dori
	Gandalf
	Nori and Ori
	Balin and Dwalin
Bofur	Bilbo
Thorin	Bilbo
	Bombur
	The dwarves
Bilbo and the dwarves	Bombur
Chief of the guards (elf)	Bilbo
Smaug	Bilbo
Bombur	Bilbo

Some examples of uses of *ja-ne* (자네) follow:

(3)
[Gandalf telling the dwarves why he had brought along Bilbo on the quest]
"After all he [Bilbo] is my friend," said the wizard, "and not a bad little chap. I feel responsible for him. I wish to goodness you had not lost him."

(*The Hobbit*: 104)

"누가 뭐라든 골목쟁이네는 내 친구라네. 그리고 나쁜 꼬마가 아니야. 난 그에 대해 책임을 느끼네. 자네들이 그를 잃어버리지 않았더라면 좋았을 것을."

(*Lee's The Hobbit*: 140)

It is interesting to note that Gandalf calls Bilbo his *chingu* (친구). Although the term can be used to describe a person that one is close to, having spent a long time with them, it is not often used in cases where one person is significantly older than the other.

(4)
[Gandalf speaking to dwarf Dori after losing Bilbo]
"Whatever did you want to go and drop him for, Dori?"

"You would have dropped him," said Dori, "if a goblin had suddenly grabbed your legs from behind in the dark, tripped up your feet, and kicked you in the back!"

(*The Hobbit*: 105)

"도대체 어쩌라고 자네는 그를 떨어뜨렸나, 도리?"
"<u>당신</u>이라도 떨어뜨렸을 겁니다. 만일 고블린이 갑자기 어둠 뒤에서 <u>당신</u> 다리를 잡은 다음 판죽을 걸고 등을 걸어찬다면요!"

(*Lee's The Hobbit*: 140)

Throughout the novel, Gandalf uses *ja-ne* (자네) to address Bilbo and the dwarves in *banmal*, but Bilbo and the dwarves address Gandalf as *dangsin* (당신), using *jeondetmal*. This highlights the asymmetrical, hierarchical relationship between these characters.

Geudae (그대) is a second-person pronoun used mainly in written Korean. It is a polite, slightly archaic way for the speaker to address a subordinate or an individual of the same age or social position. It is mostly found in songs and literary works and was only used a total of eleven times throughout the whole novel. Table 3.6 sets out who uses *geudae* (그대), and to whom.

(5)
[Letter from Thorin to Bilbo]
"Thorin and Company to Burglar Bilbo greeting! For your hospitality our sincerest thanks, and for your offer of professional assistance our grateful acceptance."

(*The Hobbit*: 35)

"소린과 일행이 좀도둑 빌보에게 인사를! <u>그대</u>의 환대에 진정으로 감사함. 그리고 <u>그대</u>가 제공하는 전문적인 도움을 감사히 수락함."

(*Lee's The Hobbit*: 58)

Thorin addresses Bilbo with *geudae* (그대) in written form; however, he predominantly uses *ja-ne* (자네) to address Bilbo in speech.

Table 3.6 Speaker and addressee where *geudae* (그대) is used in *The Hobbit*, where the hierarchical dynamic is speaker > hearer or speaker = hearer

Speaker	Addressee
Thorin	Bilbo (in a written letter) Roäc
Elves	Each other (in song)

(6)

[Thorin rejects Roäc's advice by saying the following]

Then Thorin burst forth in anger: "Our thanks, Roäc Carc's son. You and your people shall not be forgotten. But none of our gold shall thieves take or the violent carry off while we are alive. If you would earn our thanks still more, bring us news of any that draw near."

(*The Hobbit*: 289)

그러자 소린은 벌컥 화를 냈다.
"고맙소, 카르크의 아들 로악이여. <u>그대</u>와 <u>그대</u>의 종족을 잊지 않을 것
이다. 그러나 우리가 살아 있는 동안에는 도둑들이나 난폭한 자들이 우
리 황금을 빼앗거나 옮겨 갈 수 없을 것이다. 만약 <u>그대</u>가 가까이 다가온
자들의 소식을 우리에게 전해 준다면 더 고맙겠다."

(*Lee's The Hobbit*: 366)

Although Thorin is angry, he still refers to Roäc using the polite pronoun, perhaps this is because *geudae* (그대) sounds slightly less aggressive than *dangsin* (당신) when used in this manner. This pronoun selection also helps to make it clear that Thorin's anger is not directed towards Roäc himself, but rather towards those potential usurpers of whom he has been warned by Roäc.

Neo (너) is an informal pronoun used by a speaker addressing an equal or inferior; it is not a polite form of address. In the second-person plural form it becomes *neohui* (너희). Although *neo* (너), *ney* (네), and their plural forms are not used as frequently as *dangsin* (당신) in *Lee's The Hobbit*, they are used in a variety of different situations with slightly different nuances. The pronoun *ne* is used in *banmal* and is therefore used to speak casually in dialogue between close friends, family members, and younger people. It can also be used in hostile situations, including conflict, as a way of insulting the addressee. Table 3.7 sets out who uses *neo* (너), and to whom.

The fact that this is not a respectful manner of speech is clearly exemplified in the scene where Bilbo deliberately mocks the spiders in an attempt to rile up their anger, distract them, and draw them away from the dwarves, who are in imminent danger.

(7)

[Bilbo, singing to the spiders]

"Here am I, naughty little fly;
you are fat and lazy.
You cannot trap me, though you try,
in your cobwebs crazy."

(*The Hobbit*: 180)

"나는 여기 있지, 조그만 개구쟁이 파리,
너는 뚱뚱하고 게을러서

Table 3.7 Speaker and addressee where *neo* and *neohui* are used in *The Hobbit*, where the hierarchical dynamic is speaker > hearer or speaker = hearer

Speaker	Addressee
William	Bilbo Bert Tom
Tom	Bert William
Bert	Tom Bilbo William
Beorn	Bilbo Bilbo (and possibly Gandalf)
Bilbo	His sword Spiders Himself Gollum
Spiders	Bilbo
Elvenking	Thorin Balin
Galion	Group of elves
Group of guards	Bilbo and the dwarves
Thorin, Fili and Kili, and Bilbo	Group of guards
Bombur	Bilbo and the dwarves
Thorin	Fili and Kili
Smaug (dragon)	Bilbo
Bard	His arrow
Thorin	Roäc Bilbo and the dwarves Bard

아무리 해도 날 가둘 수 없지,
네 흔들리는 거미집 덫에.”

(Lee's The Hobbit: 230)

A similar sentiment is expressed in the spiders' reply to Bilbo.

(8)
[The spiders speaking to Bilbo]
"Now we see you, you nasty little creature! We will eat you and leave your bones and skin hanging on a tree. Ugh! he's got a sting, has he? Well, we'll get him all the same, and then we'll hang his head downwards for a day or two."

(The Hobbit: 182)

"이제 너를 볼 수 있다, 이 역겨운 꼬마야. 너를 먹고 네 뼈와 가죽을 나무 위에 달아 주지. 우! 침을 갖고 있군 그래? 그래도 우리는 네 놈을 잡아서 하루나 이틀 정도 머리를 거꾸로 매달아 놓을 거야."

(Lee's The Hobbit: 230)

Informal language can also be used to express particular emotions, such as anger and annoyance. Galion, for example, is irritated at a group of fellow elves who have arrived late to their duties and are behaving unprofessionally, and he uses the second-person pronoun *neohui* (너희) repeatedly to emphasise the fault of the elves' actions, instead of choosing to drop the pronouns.

(9)
[Galion to a group of elves]
"You're all late," he grumbled. "Here am I waiting and waiting down here, while you fellows drink and make merry and forget your tasks…"

(The Hobbit: 203)

"너희들 모두 늦었어. 너희들이 술을 마시고 흥겹게 놀면서 임무를 잊고 있는 동안 나는 여기 지하에서 너희들을 목 빠지게 기다렸어."

(Lee's The Hobbit: 257)

Second-person pronouns display the social status of characters in relation to each other. For example, Bilbo speaks formally to Smaug (the dragon), and refers to him with the pronoun *dangsin* (당신). Smaug, however, replies to him informally with *neo* (너) or *ne* (네). This asymmetry reflects Smaug's importance as the last "great" dragon of Middle-earth, a being who is prima facie of significantly superior status to the lowly hobbit Bilbo.

(10)
[Dialogue between Smaug and Bilbo]
"Surely, O Smaug the unassessably wealthy, you must realise that your success has made you some bitter enemies?"…
"Your information is antiquated," he snapped. "I am armoured above and below with iron scales and hard gems. No blade can pierce me."
"I might have guessed it," said Bilbo. "Truly there can nowhere be found the equal of Lord Smaug the Impenetrable. What magnificence to possess a waistcoat of fine diamonds!"

(The Hobbit: 252)

"헤아릴 수 없이 많은 보물을 소유한 자, 스마우그여, 당신의 성공으로 당신에게 원한을 품은 적들이 생겼다는 것을 알고 계시겠지요?" …
   "네가 알고 있는 정보는 케케묵은 거야. 나는 위아래로 쇠 비늘과 단단한 보석들로 무장하고 있어. 어떤 칼도 나를 뚫을 수 없다."

"그러더라도 짐작했습니다. 진정으로 꿰뚫을 수 없는 자, 스마우그 제왕 께 버금가는 자는 어디서도 찾을 수 없을 겁니다."

(Lee's The Hobbit: 316–17)

Neo (너) is also used when characters speak to inanimate objects.

(11)
[Bard speaking to his arrow]
"You have never failed me and always I have recovered you."

(The Hobbit: 279)

"너는 나를 실망시킨 적이 없었고, 언제나 나는 너를 되찾았다."

(Lee's The Hobbit: 352)

Similarly, Bilbo names his sword while he faces a dangerous situation with the spiders.

(12)
[Bilbo speaking to his sword]
"I will give you a name," he said to it, "and I shall call you Sting."

(The Hobbit: 175)

"네게 이름을 지어 주지. 너를 스팅이라고 부르겠어"

(Lee's The Hobbit: 225)

In both of these cases, the characters address their weapons with second-person pronouns. The weapons are not mere objects but treated as living companions in combat with whom they share a close, intimate relationship.

Bilbo also refers to himself using this second-person pronoun when talking to himself.

(13)
[Bilbo talking down to himself, for not be able to do more to prevent Thorin's death]
"You are a fool, Bilbo Baggins."

(The Hobbit: 323)

"너는 정말 바보야, 골목쟁이네 빌보."

(Lee's The Hobbit: 411)

Notably, these second-person pronouns are used frequently by the trolls Tom, William, and Bert when referring to each other. The three trolls are close companions, and consistently speak to each other in *banmal* alone; they predominantly refer to each other by *neo* (너) or insults. This adds to the dialogue's dynamics; the banter and the bickering between the three resemble that of a sibling relationship. However, none of the trolls use kinship terms that would reveal their relative ages or blood ties, and so the relationship between the three is not defined.

(14)
[Dialogue between Bert and William]
"You're a fat fool, William," said Bert, "as I've said before this evening."
"And you're a lout!"
"And I won't take that from you, Bill Huggins," says Bert, and puts his fist in William's eye.
Then there was a gorgeous row.

(*The Hobbit*: 43)

"너는 뚱보 바보야, 윌리엄, 아까 저녁에 말한 것처럼 말이야."
"넌 촌놈이야!"
"너한테서 그런 소리를 듣다니, 야, 빌 허긴스."
버트는 이렇게 말하며 윌리엄의 눈에 주먹을 한 방 먹었다.
곧 굉장한 싸움이 벌어졌다.

(*Lee's The Hobbit*: 67)

Despite being antagonists who are a source of potential danger to the dwarves, the trolls call each other *nom* (놈), and *meongcheonga* (멍청아) which helps to characterise the trolls as beings that are not inherently evil. Instead, they are a source of humour within the chapter, and it is their stupidity that saves the dwarves' lives. The trolls also use *nom* (놈) to refer to the dwarves that they captured after Bilbo was caught trying to steal from William's pocket. While the use of this language could add dramatic tension, instead, it is used as an outlet of humour in the novel, as shown in example 15.

(15)
[Comedic exchange between the three troll brothers discussing which dwarf to sit on and squash, so they can be cooked another time]
"The one with the yellow stockings," said Bert.
"Nonsense, the one with the grey stockings," said a voice like William's.
"I made sure it was yellow," said Bert.
"Yellow it was," said William.
"Then what did yer say it was grey for?" said Bert.
"I never did. Tom said it."
"That I never did!" said Tom. "It was you."
"Two to one, so shut yer mouth!" said Bert.
"Who are you a-talkin' to?" said William.

(*The Hobbit*: 48)

"노란 양말 신은 놈."
버트가 말했다.

"아니야 회색 양말 신은 놈이야."
윌리엄 같은 목소리로 누군가 말했다.
"틀림없이 노랑이야."
버트가 말했다.
"노란색이야."
윌리엄이 말했다.
"근데 왜 회색이라고 그랬어?"
버트가 말했다.
"난 그런 적 없어. 톰이 그랬지."
"나도 아니야. 니가 그랬지?"
톰이 말했다.
"둘 중 하나야. 니들 입 닥쳐!"
버트가 말했다.
"너 지금 누구한테 말하는 거야?"
윌리엄이 말했다.

(*Lee's The Hobbit*: 72)

3.1.4 Insulting Manner of Address

The use of *nom* (놈) is rather frequent throughout the novel, but in most cases it is not used as a direct term of address but in a descriptive manner as an adjective. *Nom* (놈) is a profanity used to degrade a male person, and *nyeon* (년) is typically considered to be the female equivalent. It cannot be used in conjunction with *jeondetmal* (it is only suitable in *banmal*), as it is a form of insult used when disrespecting someone.

(16)
[Smaug shouting out to Bilbo in an attempt to lure him out of hiding]
"Well, thief! I smell you and I feel your air. I hear your breath. Come along!"

(*The Hobbit*: 248)

"자, 도둑놈아! 네 냄새를 맡을 수 있고 네 모습을 느낄 수 있다. 네가 숨 쉬는 소리도 들린다. 이리 나와 봐라!"

(*Lee's The Hobbit*: 311)

Here, *nom* (놈) is added to the noun *doduk* (도둑; "thief") as a way of addressing Bilbo. *Doduknoma* (도둑놈아) is used in the Korean where the source text has "thief," but Korean version has become a profanity that adds an additional layer of insult and confrontation more comparable to "thieving bastard" or the like in English.

The noun *babo* (바보) can be used in a similar way to *nom* (놈), as an insult. However, it is not as disrespectful, and can be used in a light-hearted, playful manner – "idiot," "fool," or "stupid" are often given as English equivalents. There are other ways to say this in Korean such as *hogu* (호구), which is considered a more offensive term.

(17)
[Bard talking to the Elvenking about the Dain's company of dwarves]
"Fools!" laughed Bard, "to come thus beneath the Mountain's arm!"

(The Hobbit: 311)

"바보들! 산자락 아래로 오다니!"

(Lee's The Hobbit: 393)

In example 17, Bard is mocking the decision of the dwarves, and assuming they will not succeed in their endeavours to pass straight into the Mountain to fulfil their quest.

(18)
[Bilbo singing to infuriate the spiders]
"Old Tomnoddy, all big body,
Old Tomnoddy can't spy me!
Attercop! Attercop!
Down you drop!
You'll never catch me up your tree!"

(The Hobbit: 179)

"몸집만 큰 늙어진 바보야!
늙어진 바보야, 날 볼 수 없다네!
실타래! 실타래!
떨어져라!
네 나무 위에서는 나를 잡지 못할걸!"

(Lee's The Hobbit: 230)

For this song in example 18, the author translates "Old Tomnoddy" as "*neulkeojin baboya*" (늙어진 바보야). "Tomnoddy" is not a noun that is commonly used in the English language and is considered a dated expression for "a foolish or stupid person; (also) a mildly depreciative term for any person" and thus is comparable in meaning to *baboya* (바보야) (OED 2022).

(19)
[Bilbo talking to himself]
"Never laugh at live dragons, Bilbo you fool!"

(The Hobbit: 254)

"빌보 이 바보야, 다시는 살아 있는 용을 비웃지 마!"

(Lee's The Hobbit: 320)

In example 19, Bilbo is softly putting himself down for his actions after Thorin's death.

(20)

[Gandalf responding to the goblins' taunting song]

"Fly away little birds! Fly away if you can! Come down little birds, or you will get roasted in your nests! Sing, sing little birds! Why don't you sing?"

"Go away! little boys!" shouted Gandalf in answer. "It isn't bird-nesting time."

(The Hobbit: 119)

"작은 새들아, 날아 봐라! 할 수 있으면 날아가! 작은 새들아, 내려와라, 안 그러면 둥지에서 통째로 구이가 될 테니. 노래해, 노래해라, 작은 새 들아! 노래하는 게 어때?"

"꺼져, 치졸한 녀석들! 지금은 새집을 뒤질 때가 아니야."

(Lee's The Hobbit: 158)

Gandalf uses harsh language in response to the goblin's song, something that would not be expected from Gandalf, who predominantly uses respectful pronouns such as *ja-ne* (자네) when speaking to other characters who are his inferior (such as Bilbo and the dwarves). The narrator clarifies that Gandalf does this to make the goblins angry and hide his own fear.

3.1.5 *Alternative Forms of Address*

(21)

[Elves speaking to Thorin]

"Don't dip your beard in the foam, father!" they cried to Thorin, who was bent almost on to his hands and knees. "It is long enough without watering it."

(The Hobbit: 58)

"물거품에 수염을 적시지 마세요, <u>영감님</u>! 물을 안 줘도 이미 충분히 길 게 자랐으니까요."

(Lee's The Hobbit: 85)

In example 21, the elves refer to Thorin as *yeonggamnim* (영감님). This is a term used specifically to refer to an elderly man. This is an honorific term, with the suffix *nim* (님) affixed to the word *yeonggang* (영감); however, this term is not as polite as other alternatives, such as *eoreusin* (어르신).

(22)

[Balin asking a question to the Elvenking]

"What have we done, O king?"

(The Hobbit: 194)

"<u>왕이시여</u>, 우리가 무슨 잘못을 저질렀다는 말입니까?"

(Lee's The Hobbit: 244)

(23)

[Bilbo to Thorin, speaking respectfully as Thorin dies]:

"Farewell, King under the Mountain!" he said. "This is a bitter adventure, if it must end so; and not a mountain of gold can amend it."

(*The Hobbit*: 322)

"잘 가세요, 산아래의 <u>왕이시여</u>. 이렇게 끝나야 하다니, 정말 쓰라린 모험이었습니다. 황금 산을 얻는다 해도 그것을 보상할 수 없을 겁니다."

(*Lee's The Hobbit*: 411)

In examples 22 and 23, the post-positional particle *isiyeo* (이시여) is added to the noun *wang* (왕) to politely address Thorin and the Elvenking. The particle is used to express extreme respect and admiration when addressing royalty or religious figures.

3.1.6 Changes in Levels of Formality

A significant change to the level of formality in the speech between Bilbo and the dwarves can be observed if one compares their first meeting and final farewell:

(24)

[Dwalin and Bilbo meeting for the first time]

"Dwalin at your service!" he said with a low bow.

"Bilbo Baggins at yours!" said the hobbit

(*The Hobbit*: 10)

"<u>당신께 봉사하겠습니다</u>. 드왈린입니다."
"<u>당신께 봉사하겠습니다</u>. 골목쟁이네 빌보입니다."

(*Lee's The Hobbit*: 27)

(25)

[Bilbo says farewell to Dwalin and the other dwarves]

"Farewell, Balin!" he said; "and farewell, Dwalin; and farewell Dori, Nori, Ori, Oin, Gloin, Bifur, Bofur, and Bombur! May your beards never grow thin!"

(*The Hobbit*: 326)

"잘 있어요, 발린! 그리고 잘 있어요, 드왈린. 안녕히! 도리, 노리, 오리, 오인, 글로인, 비푸르, 보푸르, 봄부르! 당신들의 수염이 빠지지 않기를!"

(*Lee's The Hobbit*: 415)

The phrase "당신께 봉사하겠습니다" is used by all the dwarves when introducing themselves to Bilbo at their first meeting. The use of highly honorific language is particularly humbling. Bilbo speaks to the dwarves formally, using the honorific marker *seyo* (세요) in the first chapter; by the end of the novel, however, he drops this and speaks to them using the -*yo* (요) form. Additionally, it should be noted that, throughout the novel, pronouns are used more frequently than names as address terms; this is also the case with the dwarves and Bilbo. Thorin's company of dwarves, in particular, is often referred to as a large group – *geudeul, janedeul, dadeul, nanjaengideul, dangsindeul* (그들, 자네들, 다들, 난쟁이들, 당신들) – rather than as individuals by name. Thus, the fact that Bilbo addresses each dwarf by name in their final farewell is particularly poignant.

Another aspect to consider regarding the use of names is that in Korean, calling someone by only their given name would only be used in informal language, *banmal*. In such instances, the suffix *a* (아) is added if the name ends with a consonant or *ya* (야) if the name ends with a vowel; however, this rule does not apply to foreign names. As the book itself is foreign, and the characters are clearly not Korean, the author here translates the names as is and ignores these rules.

Bilbo's farewell is markedly different from that of Gandalf, who refers to the dwarves as a group with "다들" when saying goodbye. Gandalf also uses *banmal* consistently when speaking to these characters throughout the entire novel.

(26)
[Gandalf saying goodbye to Thorin, Bilbo, and the dwarves]
"Good-bye!" said Gandalf to Thorin. "And goodbye to you all, good-bye! Straight through the forest is your way now. Don't stray off the track! If you do, it is a thousand to one you will never find it again and never get out of Mirkwood; and then I don't suppose I, or anyone else, will ever see you again."

(The Hobbit: 156)

"소린, 잘 가게! 그리고 자네들 모두 잘 가게. 정말 조심하라고! 이제 자네들이 갈 길은 숲은 곧바로 가로지르는 거야. 길에서 벗어나기 말게. 만약 벗어나면 십중팔구 그 길을 다시 찾지도 못 할 거고 어둠숲에서도 벗어나지 못할걸세. 그러면 나나 아니면 다른 누구도 자네들을 다시는 못보게 될 거야."

(Lee's The Hobbit: 198)

(27)
[Emissaries from Dain's company of dwarves addressing the army of men and elves at the foot of the Mountain]
"But who are you that sit in the plain as foes before defended walls?" This, of course, in the polite and rather old-fashioned language of such

occasions, meant simply: "You have no business here. We are going on, so make way or we shall fight you!"

(The Hobbit: 310)

"그러나 수비된 벽 앞에 적처럼 진을 치고 있는 당신들은 누구입니까?" 이 말은 이런 경우에 공손하고 예스러운 언어로 표현되긴 했지만, 순전히 이런 뜻이었다.
"당신들은 여기서 볼일이 없다. 우리는 진군할 테니 길을 내주든가 아니면 싸우자!"

(Lee's The Hobbit: 393)

Unlike Seta or Yamamoto's Japanese translation of *The Hobbit*, there is no change in the pronouns used towards the same characters in the two levels of politeness here. The formal-polite suffix *imnida* (입니다) is used in the polite version, whereas the suffixes *da* (다) and *ja* (자) are used in the subsequent sentences. These are both informal versions of the declarative and propositional particles; their formal equivalents would be *eopsseupnida* (없습니다) and *ssaupsida* (싸웁시다). In both cases, the pronoun *dangsindul* (당신들) is used and remains unchanged.

3.2 *Harry Potter and the Philosopher's Stone*

The first volume of the Harry Potter series, *Harry Potter and the Philosopher's Stone* (Rowling 1997/2014) was translated into Korean by Kim Hyewon (김혜원; 2016). This text will be cited as *Kim's Harry Potter*. Kim (2013) admits the difficulty of translating Harry Potter at the time: "[J.K. Rowling] used lots of words that were not even in the English dictionary. The dormitory names and the names of people are often a play on archaic words, so I had to think carefully about whether to keep the words as they were or retranslate them." Kim's translations have been criticised for mistranslations of names and proper nouns as well as for misinterpretations. Of course, the *Harry Potter* series has many die-hard fans, and any translation of the series is subject to strict scrutiny. In this section we will examine the use of speech styles and their significance, and look at address terms, assessing their appropriateness.

3.2.1 *The Use of Speech Styles*

The first chapter of *Harry Potter and the Philosopher's Stone* shows an interaction between two professors: Professor McGonagall and Professor Dumbledore (*Kim's Harry Potter*: 23–32). Professor Dumbledore is older and of higher rank than Professor McGonagall. The translator takes this relationship at face value; in the Korean, Dumbledore uses a semi-formal speech style, referring to Professor McGonagall as *gyosu* (교수), or Professor, without any honorific suffixes, or as *dangsin* (당신), a neutral second-person pronoun. Professor McGonagall, in turn, refers to Professor Dumbledore as *gyosunim* (교수님), which includes the honorific suffix, and uses a higher level of speech, avoiding any second-person pronouns altogether. A portion of their dialogue follows:

(28)
DUMBLEDORE: "Fancy seeing you here, Professor McGonagall."
"여기서 <u>당신</u>을 만날 줄 알았<u>소</u>, 맥고나걸 <u>교수</u>."

MCGONAGALL: "How did you know it was me?"
"<u>저</u>라는 걸 어떻게 아<u>셨죠</u>?"

DUMBLEDORE: "My dear Professor, I've never seen a cat sit so stiffly."
"이봐요, <u>교수</u>. 난 그렇게 뻣뻣이 앉아 있는 고양이는 본 적이 없<u>어요</u>."

MCGONAGALL: "You'd be stiff if you'd been sitting on a brick wall all day."
"<u>교수님</u>도 벽돌담 위에 온종일 앉아 있었다면 그렇게 뻣뻣해졌을 거<u>예요</u>."

DUMBLEDORE: "All day? When you could have been celebrating? I must have passed a dozen feasts and parties on my way here."
"온종일이라<u>고요</u>? 그럼 축하할 겨를도 없었겠<u>구려</u>? 난 여기 오는 길에 축제와 파티를 수십 번은 거쳤을 <u>거요</u>."

MCGONAGALL: "Oh yes, everyone's celebrating, all right."
"아, 그러<u>시겠죠</u>. 모두가 축제 기분에 젖어 있<u>군요</u>, 좋<u>아요</u>."

(*Harry Potter*: 10; *Kim's Harry Potter*: 23)

The English reader must use contextual clues to gradually discover more about the relationship between Professors McGonagall and Dumbledore. The fact that Dumbledore outranks McGonagall is alluded to, but the reader does not learn this outright until later in the story. In Korean, however, the reader is immediately informed that McGonagall defers to Dumbledore, though the reason for that deference is not made clear quite as quickly. the Korean reader can also see from the way Dumbledore addresses McGonagall that he is respectful towards her, although he obviously outranks her in some way.

This dialogue between Dumbledore and McGonagall is an accurate portrayal of speech styles in Korean, though it seems fairly robotic in its exactness (real speech styles tend to vary based on context and levels of intimacy – a person is likely to use many kinds of speech styles in any given interaction).

Example 29 is another example of speech styles as translated in the story, this time between the main character Harry Potter's uncle Vernon and his wife Petunia:

(29)
VERNON: "Petunia, dear – you haven't heard from your sister lately, have you?"
"페투니아, <u>당신</u> 최근에 동생 소식 못 들었<u>소</u>?"

PETUNIA: "No... Why?"
"아뇨...왜<u>요</u>?"

VERNON: "Funny stuff on the news... and there were a lot of funny-looking people in town today..."
"뉴스에 우스꽝스러운 얘기가 나와서...그리고 오늘 시내에는 이상하게 보이는 사람들이 많이 있었<u>거든</u>..."

PETUNIA: "So?"
"그래서<u>요</u>?"

VERNON: "Well, I just thought... maybe... it was something to do with... you know... her crowd... Their son – he'd be about Dudley's age now, wouldn't he?"
"글쎄, 난 그저...어쩌면...그게 말<u>이야</u>..., 그 집 식구들과 어떤 관계가 있는 게 아닌가 해서 말<u>이야</u>....그 집 아들 말<u>이야</u>.... 그 애도 지금쯤 두들리 나이 정도 됐겠지, 안 <u>그래</u>?"

PETUNIA: "I suppose so."
"그렇겠<u>죠</u>."

(*Harry Potter*: 7–8; *Kim's Harry Potter*: 19–20)

Here, Vernon (the husband) is seen using a lower speech level (closest to the "semi-formal style" described earlier) to his wife – he mostly uses half-talk endings (*ya*/야, *ji*/지, etc.) with some slightly more formal styles (*so*/소). Petunia, on the other hand, uses more respectful, deferential language to her husband. This dynamic is culturally accurate; many Korean couples converse in this way with each other. Like the interaction between the two professors, this interaction would not feel awkward to a Korean reader. However, the usage of speech styles portrayed here is fairly idealistic – this is how a husband and wife are *supposed* to speak to each other. It may be more representative of real-world relationships to show greater variety in the speech styles used – most Korean couples now do not follow this rigid pattern (Kiaer 2020b: 16).

Interactions in the text between children and adults also tend to follow a set, textbook pattern. Adults are always seen using half-talk with children, and children are always seen using formal language with adults. Example 30 contains some dialogue between Professor Snape, who is considered as a particularly nasty character, with one of the children at Hogwarts School of Witchcraft and Wizardry:

(30)
SNAPE: "What would I get if I added powdered root of asphodel to an infusion of wormwood?"
"쑥을 우려낸 물에 수선화 뿌리를 갈아 넣으면 뭐가 되<u>지</u>?"

HARRY: "I don't know, sir."
"전 모르겠는데<u>요</u>."

SNAPE: "Tut, tut – fame clearly isn't everything... Let's try again. Potter, where would you look if I told you to find me a bezoar?"
"쯧쯧...확실히 이름값을 못하는군...다시 한 번 해보<u>자</u>. 포터, 위석을 찾으려면 어디를 봐야 하<u>지</u>?"

HARRY: "I don't know, sir."
"모르겠는데<u>요</u>."

SNAPE: "Thought you wouldn't open a book before coming, eh, Potter?"
"넌 오기 전에 책도 한번 들춰 보지 않았<u>니</u>, 포터?"

(*Harry Potter*: 146–7; *Kim's Harry Potter*: 196–7)

The professor's use of the sentence ending particles -*ji* (지) and -*ni* (니) contrast with Harry's use of the formal -*yo* (요). Though it is not improper for Snape to use informal sentence endings, as he is a teacher of higher status than his students, the content of what Snape says helps the Korean reader to know how the speech style is being used. In this case, the informal speech endings emphasise the nasty nature of Snape's speech.

In the translated text, children tend to always use half-talk with other children, even upon a first meeting, regardless of age. Example 31 sets out the dialogue of two children who have just met for the first time:

(31)
DRACO: "Hello... Hogwarts, too?"
"안녕..." 너도 호그와트<u>니</u>?"

HARRY: "Yes."
"<u>요</u>."

DRACO: "My father's next door buying my books and mother's up the street looking at wands... Have you got your own broom?"
"우리 아빠는 옆 가게에서 내 책을 사고 계시고 엄마는 길가에서 요술지팡이를 보고 계<u>셔</u>... 넌 빗자루 있<u>니</u>?"

HARRY: "No."
"<u>아니</u>."

(*Harry Potter*: 83; *Kim's Harry Potter*: 116)

This immediate use of half-talk without any negotiation is not unusual for children of the same age, so it does not come across as unnatural here. The speech styles used in the translation shown are, again, appropriate and acceptable to the target culture (they were translated by a native Korean speaker, so they naturally follow the rules of appropriate speech styles). However, they do not perhaps do as well at portraying realistic dynamics in relationships. Actual speech style is determined as much by intimacy as it is by social hierarchy. A more varied, less prescriptive approach to speech styles might make the relationships in the book feel more real. That being said, the speech styles shown are typically culturally appropriate and would not come across as strange to the Korean reader.

When children of different ages interact, something similar can be observed. In the example that follows, Fred Weasley speaks to Oliver Wood, who is older than Fred. Fred uses an honorific speech style, but addresses Oliver by his name, rather than *yeong*, the typical address term for an older boy. Meanwhile, Oliver uses informal speech, *banmal*, and informal address terms, as he is Fred's senior:

(32)

FRED: "We know Oliver's speech by heart," Fred told Harry, "we were on the
　　　team last year."
　　　"우리는 올리버의 연설을 진심으로 압니다. 우리는 작년에 그 팀에
　　　있었습니다."

OLIVER: "Shut up, you two," said Wood. "This is the best team Gryffindor's
　　　had in years. We're going to win. I know it."
　　　"닥쳐, 너희 둘. 이 팀은 몇 년 동안 그리핀도르가 가진 최고의 팀이야.
　　　우리가 이길거야. 나도 알아."

　　　　　　　　　　　　　　　(*Harry Potter*: 198; *Kim's Harry Potter*: 239)

Thus, although speech between children is often translated in an orthodox way, Kim does allude to the fact that Fred is a cheeky character by having him use the first name of someone older than him. In this way, there is still some nuance within Kim's translation, even if it may not be abundant.

Table 3.8 provides an overview of the textbook conventions in the translation of Harry Potter discussed in this section.

3.2.2 *Appropriate and Inappropriate Use of Address Terms*

The translation of *Harry Potter* is full of examples of translated address terms, which seem to have posed a greater problem for the translator than speech styles. Some address terms are used in very culturally appropriate ways, such as *gyosunim* (교수님) as shown earlier. Various kinship terms are also used.

Harry lives with his aunt Petunia, uncle Vernon, and cousin Dudley. The story specifies that the aunt is Harry's mother's sister, so Harry refers to his uncle as *imobu* (이모부) (*Kim's Harry Potter*: 96), which is the precise address term that would be used for this relationship in natural Korean. His uncle and aunt frequently refer to each other as *yeobo* (여보) (*Kim's Harry Potter*: 69), which is also an accurate address term for a husband and wife to use to address

Table 3.8 An overview of textbook conventions in the Korean translation of *Harry Potter and the Philosopher's Stone*

Status of interlocutors	Rules governing speech styles	Representative examples
Adults to Adults	Always hierarchy-based	Dumbledore uses semi-formal with McGonagall. McGonagall uses formal/polite with Dumbledore.
Adults to children	Always *banmal*	Snape uses formal language when teaching, but *banmal* to each individual child.
Children to adults	Always formal/polite	Harry uses polite language to all professors.
Children to children	Always *banmal*, regardless of age	Harry and classmates use *banmal* to all other students.
Husband to wife	Wife shows deference	Vernon uses semi-formal or *banmal* to Petunia, Petunia uses formal to Vernon.

each other. The uncle and aunt consistently address Harry and his cousin by name, which is appropriate for adults when speaking to children.

Other families are also shown using culturally appropriate address terms. The Weasley family prominently features in the story, and includes a mother, father, and several children. In a nuclear family, Korean address terms follow strict rules, and the translation follows those rules fairly closely; Mrs Weasley calls her children by name, they call her *oemma* (엄마), the older children address the younger children by name, and the younger children use appropriate address terms for the older children (Fred and George, who are twins, call their older brother Percy *peosi hyeong* (퍼시 형)) (*Kim's Harry Potter*: 142).

Outside of families, too, address terms are used in a way that corresponds fairly closely to target-culture norms. Children address other children in their year by name, and teachers use the children's names as well. However, there are also many examples of address terms being used in this translation in ways that are blatantly foreign and culturally inappropriate (in the target culture). For example, Vernon and Petunia, a middle-aged married couple, are seen calling each other by name (65), and children are seen calling adults by name as well – Harry and others call the school gamekeeper, who is an adult man, by his last name, Hagrid (e.g., 90). Such an action would cause extreme contention in a real Korean interaction. Even in the first chapter, where Professor McGonagall and Professor Dumbledore use such rigidly correct speech styles with each other, at one point Professor McGonagall breaks from her pattern and calls Professor Dumbledore by his first name, Albus, with no title (*Kim's Harry Potter*: 26).

Harry seems to refer to his cousin, Dudley, by name, even though Dudley is several months his senior (within extended families, address terms are used strictly even by children born in the same year). Fred and George Weasley are twins, but Fred is older – and still, we see George call him by his first name with no address term (140). A vocative particle is only added to a name one time in the entire first volume, when Harry's uncle calls his name and adds the *ya* (야) particle (61). The particle may either imply affection from an adult to a child, or, perhaps, was used to show the hierarchy between Harry and his uncle: Harry is of a markedly lower status. This way of addressing Harry is not repeated anywhere in the book, even by the same character. To an English speaker, such examples may seem unimportant or trivial, but the inconsistency would never naturally occur in conversation between two Korean people in the same circumstances.

The question of address terms in translation is not an easy one; the characters in *Harry Potter* are British, not Korean, so there is the underlying awareness that they would not follow Korean rules of address terms with each other in the source text. However, when their interactions are translated into Korean for a Korean audience, and Korean rules of address terms are not followed, the readers may feel uncomfortable or disengaged. Regardless, thousands of Koreans are exposed to this kind of translation of English media. Speech styles are represented accurately, but address terms are used in a very non-traditional manner. A Korean person who reads about Harry addressing an adult man, Hagrid, by name, may not feel uncomfortable themselves addressing a foreigner by name in real life. Whether there is any sort of causal relationship there is unclear, but the way such a popular English text has been translated seems to be indicative of a prevailing attitude about using address terms with foreigners.

Table 3.9 lays out the use of address terms in the book. Some address terms make total sense, and notably, they are often related to the familial structure. Others, however, appear inappropriate and misinformed.

3.3 Conclusion

In this chapter, we have once again seen the difficulty of translating English texts into a highly context-dependent language. Our findings demonstrate that translations are dependent on (1) the translator intrinsically understanding the nature of relationships between characters, and (2) the style and tone that the translator would like to adopt. As seen with Japanese in Chapter 2, translators of *The Hobbit* and *Harry Potter* tend to be influenced by English's ample use of the second-person pronouns, and as such, we find an unusual amount of second-person pronouns in the Korean translations. There are also plenty of instances where address terms are translated questionably. In some cases, like *ja-ne*, they may stylistically emphasise the fantasy nature of the work and provide an eccentric feeling to the characters. In other cases, like in *Harry Potter*, address terms seem to be used inappropriately for the context. Even though there may be an understanding between reader and translator that this is a foreign text, it can be jarring to suddenly find characters using address terms that are highly inappropriate in the target culture. The conflicting priorities

Table 3.9 An overview of the use of terms of address and the purpose for their use in the Korean translation of *Harry Potter and the Philosopher's Stone*

Speaker	Addressee	Term of Address	Purpose
Ron Weasley	Older brothers	*Hyeong* (형)	Hierarchy
Fred and George Weasley	Percy (older brother)	*Hyeong* (형)	Hierarchy
Vernon/Petunia	Petunia/Vernon	*Yeobo* (여보)	Husband/wife
Vernon	Petunia	Name	Inappropriate usage
Professor McGonagall	Albus Dumbledore ("Albus")	Name	Inappropriate usage
Harry Potter	Hagrid	Name	Inappropriate usage
Harry Potter	Dudley	Name	Inappropriate usage
George Weasley	Fred Weasley	Name	Inappropriate usage
Children	Other children	Name	Equality
Adults	Children	Name	Seniority
Students	Teachers	Professional term of address (e.g., *gyosunim* (교수님))	Hierarchy
Teachers	Teachers	Professional term of address	Respect/humility
Mr Ollivander	Harry Potter	*Jane* (자네)	
Strangers	Harry Potter	*Jane* (자네)	
Albus Dumbledore	Professor McGonagall	*Neo* (너)	Hierarchy
Vernon	Petunia	*Neo* (너)	Husband/wife
Hagrid	Vernon	*Neo* (너)	Confrontation

involved in balancing the style of the source text and the expectations in the target culture mean that the translator takes on a huge task. They need to know the book just as well as the author does, but they need to find details that the author may not feel are essential to relay in an obvious way. The result is a text influenced by the translator's personal awareness of the interpersonal structures within the texts.

4   Fan Translation

The advent of the World Wide Web and then social media in the past three decades has brought about a massive shift in translation culture – perhaps the most significant shift in centuries. The Internet has revolutionised how translations can be produced and distributed. A publisher is no longer necessary for a translation to reach a wide readership; fan translators can now upload subtitle files, ROM hacks, eBooks, or translation notes and explanations (for video media, video games, books, or other forms of media). While many of these forms of unofficial translations can be legally dubious or outright illegal, they now form an undeniably important part of the translation landscape online, and the existence of alternate translations for media whose translations are usually tightly controlled by copyright holders can sometimes be of benefit to consumers of translated media.

When it comes to the production side, the Internet has also enabled new forms of decentralised collaboration that challenge many of our established assumptions about translation. Those with knowledge of a language can easily coordinate online to form organised translation teams that are often spread across numerous countries and time zones, often working for free. Often, multiple different teams of fan translators will produce competing unofficial translations of the same media, allowing for multiple interpretations of the same media to coexist beyond the one official translation usually provided by copyright holders.

Ordinary people are now able to contribute their own translations of source texts they are passionate about, contributing to a richer and more diverse range of available translations. Some of these translations may be rougher or more awkward than any translation that would be accepted for publication – yet these unpolished or offhand translations may reveal some facet of the meaning of a text that would be polished away in a smoother translation.

The sheer abundance of information that characterises the current Internet age, particularly following the mass adoption of social media, means that there is far more text in need of translation. Even the most seemingly trivial of texts, such as comments under a YouTube video, may be deemed worthy of translation to many who encounter them. As a result, we find ourselves in need of ephemeral, offhand translations to match the offhand texts we encounter

DOI: 10.4324/9781003217466-4

online. Tools like Google Translate are perfect for tasks like these – even if machine translation may never reach the level of quality and nuance provided by a professional translator, the rough translations they can instantly provide for us now is often enough for our online needs. Online discussions between multilingual participants are often mediated by these tools, which, even if they are imperfect, allow for enough of an understanding to facilitate discussions.

In short, the present era of translation is one characterised by decentralisation, speed, and a lack of barriers. The ease with which translations can be distributed online has provided audiences for translations that may not meet traditional criteria for professional translation, while disrupting the hegemony of copyright holders by providing the option to choose from multiple competing unofficial translations. This huge shift in translation culture has occurred incredibly quickly – within the last twenty-to-thirty years – and it seems likely that translation will continue to become more decentralised and open in the coming years.

This chapter explores some of the key aspects of media translation by fans, particularly in popular culture. The examples we will look at include manga, manhwa, anime, and webtoons, and K-pop.

4.1 What Is Fan Translation?

Fan translation refers to the unofficial translation of a variety of forms of text – be they written or multimedia products – by fans rather than professionals. Typically, this type of translation is performed by fans because an official translation is not available yet. Unlike commercial translations, which are made for financial gain, fan translations are made for different reasons. Commonly these translations are performed as a form of participation within a fan community; they are not only a practical solution to the problem of a lack of access to a professional translation (or delays in such access deemed unacceptable to the fan community) but a means of bonding and creating solidarity. In fact, this is not only participation as a means of membership, but in many cases literally "communal translation," in which fans work in teams to translate and recreate the graphic elements to accommodate the translation.

Fan translation or "fanlation" started in the 1990s on the Internet. Driven by a desire to play Japanese games that were winning awards yet rarely being translated into other languages, fans began translating video games through game console emulators. One example is the role-playing video game *Eiyū Densetsu* (Japanese) known in English as *The Legend of Heroes*, which was first released in 1989 as a part of Nihon Falcom Corporation's *Dragon Slayer* game franchise in *Dragon Slayer: The Legend of Heroes*. Since then, fans have actively participated in the translation of other texts. Famous examples include books from the celebrated *Harry Potter* series by J.K. Rowling, which have been translated by fandoms prior to the official release of commercial translations.

4.1.1 Types of Fan Translation

There are a variety of types of fan translation and several terms used to describe them. This section will provide definitions of some of the most common.

"Scanlation" is a form of translation most common for the translation of *manga* (see Figure 4.1). This trendy term is a portmanteau of "scan" and "translation," taken from this particular process, which involves scanning the pages of the comic or graphic novel, performing various operations such as adjusting the contrast and erasing source language text, and translating the text for insertion into the blank spaces. This is often conducted without copyright permission.

Then there is the "fansubbing" of multimedia products, which involves translating the subtitles. Unlike the translation of comics and graphic novels, fansubbing is often created by a single translator (rather than a group), to provide access to other fans who might not speak the source language. "Fandubbing" is like fansubbing but, instead of translating the subtitles, fans provide dubbing so that viewers can hear the dialogue in their own language.

4.1.2 Importance of Fan Translation: Popular Culture and Globalisation

Fan translation has extended the reach that texts typically have, resulting in the sharing of popular culture among larger numbers of people and more diverse groups, creating a greater sense in of membership in a global community. J.K. Rowling's *Harry Potter* is again an ideal example, having been translated into over eighty languages, partly through fan translations. Readers of the books have shared knowledge of the stories, and this common knowledge acts as a form of social currency upon which online communities can form regardless of traditional linguistic or cultural boundaries. In many ways, fan participation (including translation) through social media has paved the way for a global landscape in which, because of technological advances and the widespread adoption of such technologies, online communities are fast becoming primary as on- and offline realities merge into one.

Fan translations are in many cases breaches of copyright law, and the activity is capable of causing many harms. These include depriving those involved in the creation of the original work of the benefits that rightfully belong to them, and thereby damaging the industries that fans depend on for the content they love so much. In an ideal world, translations of content would be immediately available in all of the world's languages, supporting a thriving industry of professional translators, with consumers able to critique and comment on translations to their hearts' content. Nevertheless, and with the caveat that the benefits do not justify the harms or breaking the law, it is an ill wind that blows nobody any good, and fan translations have brought some positive impacts. As well as its role in the formation of global communities, fan translation may provide benefits in terms of popularising traditional texts, preserving endangered languages, and enhancing diversity. Traditional works, can be given a new lease of life in new domains, potentially providing the opportunity to bring them back into circulation, whether it be encouraging these texts to be re-read or stimulating new conversations surrounding these texts within current cultural or political contexts. Fan translation is incredibly beneficial to minorities not only in making texts accessible to them, but also in preserving endangered languages by, for instance, translating popular franchises such as *Harry Potter* into rare languages like Maori. Thus, fan translation is not only a tool for carving out a global terrain, but for preserving individual cultures and languages. By making culture and popular cultural products accessible, fan translation has played a role in increasing diversification. Fan translation is likely to have paved the way for East Asian traditional and popular culture becoming increasingly accessible in the mainstream around the globe. Netflix is one example of a mainstream provider, which is taking advantage of the awareness of and openness to East Asian products that is made clear in the interests of viewers and mainstream news.

4.2 Manga, Manhwa, Anime, and Webtoon Translation

This section will discuss specifically the fan translation of webtoons, and electronic manga, manhwa, and anime, focusing on the difficulties often encountered in their translation, the methods translators use for overcoming them, and the importance of the routes chosen for doing so.

4.2.1 What's the Difference between Manga, Manhwa, Anime, and Webtoons?

To begin, it would be pertinent to explain briefly what manga, manhwa, anime, and webtoons are. Anime is a form of animation originating from Japan, which may be produced by hand or through computer animation. In Japan, the term *anime* is used to describe all animation regardless of style or origin; outside of Japan, however, it is used to refer specifically to Japanese animation. Manga are comics or graphic novels originating from Japan. Most conform to a style developed in Japan in the late nineteenth century. The term *manga* is also used in Japan to refer generally to comics and the art of cartooning, while outside of Japan the word is used to refer to specifically Japanese comics. Manhwa are South Korean comics and graphic novels. Both the terms *manga* and *manhwa* come from the Chinese term *manhua*, which means "impromptu drawings." The creators of these East Asian comics also have specific titles: a person who makes manga is a *mangaka*, a person who creates manhwa is a *manhwaga*, and a person that makes manhua is a *manhuajia*. Webtoons are full colour, digital comics, serially released in episodes, with roots in the digitally published amateur web comics of the 1990s that were originally hosted on personal sites because they could not be published by mainstream manhwa magazines. In their e-form, manga and manhwa differ from webtoons in that they are scanned (and generally black and white) pages, while webtoons are read by scrolling.

4.2.2 The Importance of Emotional Equivalence

The term "emotional equivalence" is coined here to refer to the intended equivalence involved in the expression of emotion in the target text to convey an expression of emotion in the source text, and the hypothesis put forward in this chapter that emotional equivalence is a primary goal of fan translation. This is demonstrated in the creative freedom translators seem to have when selecting equivalents for gesture, vocal behaviour, terms of address, interjections, onomatopoeia, and culturally specific items; fan translators generally seem averse to naturalising strategies that would detract from conveying the emotion expressed by a given character in the source text.

4.2.3 Address Terms

Having looked at address terms in Chapters 2 and 3, let us begin with address terms here. Chapters 2 and 3 demonstrated the wider repertoire, and greater specificity, of address terms in Korean and Japanese than in English. Translating from English to those languages therefore tends to involve the introduction of pragmatic meaning that may not be explicit or restricted to such narrow interpretation in the source text. Translating from Korean and Japanese to natural English, on the other hand, can easily involve the loss of these more specific and explicit pragmatic meanings, which fan translators are often hesitant to accept. We will now look at some examples, showing strategies available to translators when dealing with address terms.

Yumi's Cells, *Ep. 3, "Stop it"*

First, there is the option of romanising the address term instead of transferring it to its nearest equivalent. Figure 4.1 presents an example of such an occasion.

The excerpt in Figure 4.1 appears early in the highly popular webtoon *Yumi's Cells*. In the scene, new recruit Ruby is meeting Wook, a co-worker and Yumi's current crush. Ruby has just interrupted Wook and Yumi's conversation, which leads Yumi to use *oppa* in order to stress the intimacy between her and Wook (despite barely knowing him) in front of Ruby. Her forthrightness is important because the rivalry between Yumi and Ruby is central to the plot of the next few episodes, but it is also important to the emotional context of the scene, with impacts on other characters than the speaker. Yumi's use of the address term *oppa* after only just having met Wook can be expected to make him (and the reader) feel uncomfortable; it can even be considered cringeworthy.

In order to create emotional equivalence, the relational dynamics of this term are needed, but *oppa* is difficult to translate into English. An equivalent in English might be "mate," but it would not express the same level of

Figure 4.1 Ruby introduces herself to Wook (English translation, left; Korean ori-
    ginal, right) in *Yumi's Cells*
Source: Lee 2015–20.

intimacy as *oppa*; it also disregards the junior–senior and female–male
relations expressed by the term and removes the flirty connotation that *oppa*
has when used by girls in contexts like this. The Translator's Note (TN) is
an effective solution, but reliance on paratextual material like this, which is
frequent on webtoon and K-drama online fanbases, shows the difficulty in
translating *oppa*. This preference for the romanised Korean might explain
why the Japanese fan translations (Figure 4.2) also often approach translation in this way, despite there being more appropriate equivalents for *oppa*
in Japanese. Although this could also simply be the result of Japanese fan
translators consulting the official English translation, rather than the Korean
source, when making their translation.[1]

The Boxer, *Ep. 40*

In the episode of *The Boxer* shown in Figure 4.3, a child is introduced to
a friend of his father. In the source text, he calls her *ajumeoni* (아주머니),
a politer form of *ajumma,* an address term used to address a middle-aged
woman who one does not know well and who does not hold a particularly
high social position. The woman is insulted by this term, because it makes her
sound older than she feels , so she scolds him and tells him to call her *nuna*
(누나; "big sister") instead, a term used by younger males to address older
females.

  There is clearly difficulty translating into French (top-left) and English
(top-right), due to a lack of appropriate equivalents. The French translator chooses the address term "madame" (traditionally referring to a
married woman and also used to address an older woman) in opposition to

Figure 4.2 Ruby introduces herself to Wook (Japanese translation) in *Yumi's Cells*
Source: Lee 2015–20.

Figure 4.3 A young boy greets his father's female friend (French, left; English, middle; Korean, right) in *The Boxer*
Source: Ji-Hoon 2019.

"mademoiselle" (traditionally referring to an unmarried woman and also used to address a younger woman) as an insult, and the English translator chooses "old woman." The former ("madame") isn't as affective as an insult as *ajumeoni*, but it does provide a more senior term in contrast to the younger that "mademoiselle" that "madame" is corrected to. The latter ("old lady") isn't an address term at all but a way to either refer to or describe an elderly woman, and can also used as an insult; this feels unnatural and comes across as intentionally rude, which is not the intended purpose in the source text. Both are clearly chosen because they express an older rather than younger age, and this is vital if the "insult" felt by the hearer is to be interpreted, thus showing the importance to the translator of expressing the insult or "emotion" (hurt feelings in this case).

Yakitate!! Japan, *Ep. 1, 6:10*

In the scene shown in Figure 4.4, a daughter (and the sister of the main character) is asking her mother if they can have bread for breakfast instead of rice.

Figure 4.4 A mother addresses her daughter at breakfast in *Yakitate!! Japan*
Source: Aoki 2004–6.

The start of the conversation goes as follows (English subtitles in brackets):

DAUGHTER: *māmā* (マーマー) ("mum/mummy").
MOTHER: *okāchan to ii, keshikiwarui* (お母ちゃんといい、気色悪い) ("That's displeasing, call me *Okaa-chan*").

English does not have neat equivalents for the two address terms for one's mother as found in this conversation in the source text. It could certainly be argued that "mum" or "mummy" is more casual than "mother," but it would be strangely formal (although possible) for a mother to insist on being called "mother." The request to be called *okaa-chan* also would not easily support such a translation, as the mother's preference for the affectionate suffix *-chan* shows that she is not being cold or distant towards her daughter. What the mother actually disapproves of is the use of the katakana word, a trend among youth, much like the sister's request to eat bread rather than rice for breakfast. If one tried to translate this dichotomy in terms of "mum" and "mother," then we would lose the core meaning of the mother's desire for her children to adhere to more traditional Japanese practices rather than behaviours she sees as more foreign.

As demonstrated in the earlier example with *oppa,* the address term from the source text has been retained in the translation (in romanised form) in an effort to ensure transparency with respect to the emotion of the parties involved. There is the sense that natural target-language options are insufficient. In this case, the emotional equivalence pertains to the mother – ensuring that she is not misunderstood as distant and cold, but rather as well-humoured and simply attempting to instruct her daughter as to the more traditional norms that she believes to be more wholesome (as opposed to modern foreign influences).

Yakitate!! Japan, *Ep. 4, 4:20*

In the scene depicted in Figure 4.5, the main character, Kazuma, has just been employed at a bakery in south Tokyo. He has already met the company head's granddaughter and speaks about their meeting. However, he lacks manners, and speaks using very casual terms of address. He uses *koitsu* to refer to the granddaughter and doesn't attach *-san* to her name. Another employee hears him speak like this and exclaims in surprise, "*ē, 'koitsu' yabai*" (えー、'こいつ'やばい).

There isn't any close English equivalent for *koitsu*. The very visible reaction of the other employee would be very confusing without some explanation of this problematic term having been used, however, which makes omission difficult even for a translator who might have otherwise preferred such an option. The translator in this case has used a translator's note, conforming with the strategy already seen in the earlier example of *oppa*. This is only one

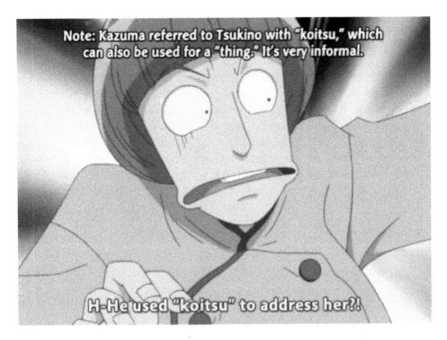

Figure 4.5 Kazuma's co-worker is shocked at his informality in *Yakitate!! Japan*
Source: Aoki 2004–6.

of several instances where Kazuma uses impolite, male language in situations where it is normal to be more formal, and there are multiple occasions where the strangeness of his language is commented upon. In all these instances, the impolite language is not used because Kazuma is trying to be insulting, but rather to express his simple mindedness, frank nature, and intensity. It would be difficult to use existing target-language alternatives that could allow both the interpretation of rudeness by colleagues and an interpretation of uncultured honesty by readers. This case is tied to emotional equivalence because rudeness suggests a negative or hostile emotion towards the granddaughter, but the speaker's emotion is actually more positive. Using a translator's note is once again seen as the safest option for achieving emotional equivalence.

4.2.4 Interjections

Interjections in Japanese anime and manga are less difficult to translate than address terms. This is mainly because they are very rarely loaded with meaning that cannot be found elsewhere; furthermore, the fact that anime and manga are famed for their very expressive characters can make extremely bold and unusual target-text language less difficult to accept.

Sleepy Princess in the Demon Castle *(魔法城でお休み)*, *Ep. 12, 7:36*

In this scene, two characters are shocked that the princess' own mother is unable to recognise that they have replaced her with a body double that looks nothing like the princess. When they are shocked they exclaim *sugō* (スゴ) and the subtitles register this as "Shocked!" (Figure 4.6). Using an adjective like this is a common way to convey the interjection, getting the meaning across at the expense of sounding unnatural in English. The hyper-expressivity of the characters reduces the level of sensitivity surrounding these interjections, making outlandish translations such as this less subject to criticism. In this case, the image accompanying the interjection shows the characters' legs pointing in the air: a comedic anime shorthand for falling over in shock. Added to expressive facial reactions before and after the interjection, the idea is easy enough for foreign audiences to grasp.

From the perspective of emotional equivalence, it can be seen that where the emotional context of the source is clearer, there is less difficulty in translation.

Cheese in Trap, *Ep. 5*

The panel in Figure 4.7 shows the protagonist Hong Seol talking about someone who paid for her dinner earlier in the day. Her friend is worried that she has been leaching off their mutual friend Euntaek again, so she accuses Hong of forcing him to pay for her. Hong is annoyed because recently she herself had to pay Euntaek's bill. As such, she says, in exasperation, that Euntaek didn't pay for her and in fact he's the one making her pay for things. Her friend is then excited by this new mystery man who has paid for the Hong's meal.

Figure 4.6 The queen fails to recognise her own daughter in *Sleepy Princess in the Demon Castle*
Source: Yamazaki 2020.

Figure 4.7 Seol's friend wants to know about the new boy (Korean, left; English, right) in *Cheese in Trap*

Source: Soonkki 2010.

The interjection *heol* (헐) feels awkward when translated in English. As a standalone interjection, one could try options such as "god!" or "hell no!" – phrases that emphasise shock at what is being said. However, the multimodal expressions that are combined with "*heol*" – the position of *heol* outside of the speech bubble, the four lines in an inverted square to show anger and the sweat drops to show exasperation – make *heol* more of a complex proposition. Having been separated from the verbal elements in the speech bubble, *heol* (along with the illustrative elements) is a way for the audience to understand the tone of the verbal elements. "Gosh" doesn't really convey this tone of shock, and adopting a strategy such as that in the previous example, with "shocked" or "shock," would read unnaturally because these are not typical interjections in English (the source text here does not approach the hyperexpressivity of the previous example, and so such a strategy would involve a change in the tone of the text).

4.2.5 Onomatopoeia and Other Ideophones

Japanese and Korean both have more fully developed ideophonic systems than English. Indeed, the word onomatopoeia itself underserves the systems in Korean and Japanese, where words exist to reflect the nature of states or actions that involve no sound; these include psychomimes, which convey mental states or attitudes, and phenomimes, which convey non-auditory states or conditions (such as the fluffiness of a cloud, for example). Ideophones are sometimes translated using verbs or adjectives. This is common in action series such as *The Boxer*. But they tend to lose their intended playfulness or to be an imperfect fit. They are also sometimes transliterated from the source-text original, though this loses the potentially significant difference between the choice in Japanese of whether to use katakana or hiragana script. Transliteration also presents the risk of confusion where the sound symbolism varies from language to language.

Cheese in Trap *and* Yumi's Cells*, Ep. 13:* 힉

Figures 4.8 and 4.9 show two such examples, with translations of the same ideophone from *Cheese in Trap* and *Yumi's Cells*. In *Cheese in Trap*, the protagonist is lost in thought while being invited out by her friends to a café. She is busy staring at her love interest, still uncertain what to make of the mixed signals he has been sending. When he notices her staring, 힉 (*hic*) is used to convey that she is surprised and taken aback. In *Yumi's Cells*, Yook, the main love interest, has just woken up after a night of drinking and can't remember what happened. Upon getting to the office, Ruby (Yumi's love rival) jumps on Yook to remind him about a drunken plan they made to go to the flower festival. Yook had completely forgotten about this plan, and 힉 is used to express his surprise.

In the English translation of *Cheese in Trap* the verb "yoink" is used. However, this suggests that the protagonist is being pulled by the arm over her shoulder rather than surprised by a man's stare. Meanwhile, the literal romanisation "hic" in *Yumi's Cells* can be interpreted as the sound a drunk person makes – this usage can be seen generally in Western cartoons. Moreover, given that the character just woke up with a massive hangover and could plausibly still be drunk, using the "hic" sound here could lead to the reader to quite a different interpretation than given by the source text. Yook's surprise is not a likely interpretation, in any case.

This is not to say that a satisfactory translation is impossible or that the meanings conveyed in the source cannot be transmitted to English-language readers. In the case of *Cheese in Trap*, the clear widening of eyes shows that the protagonist is shocked and taken aback. As for *Yumi's Cells* there is a

Figure 4.8 Hong Seol is surprised when Yu Jung notices her staring (Korean, left; English, right) in *Cheese in Trap*

Source: Soonkki 2010.

Figure 4.9 Yook is taken aback by Ruby's desperate invitation (Korean, left; English, right) in *Yumi's Cells*

Source: Lee 2015–20.

perspiration drop and an exploding yellow bubble, which are internationally recognised signs for comic readers. That is to say, the helpful cues provided by the images themselves mean that, in these two instances, the readers are likely to understand that the characters in question are experiencing some form of surprise.

Yumi's Cells, *Ep. 15*

In the example shown in Figure 4.10, Yumi's so-called anxiety cell is playfully making her anxious over what clothes to wear on her date with Yook. The cell's legs beat in the air with a 덩가一덩가一 (*dingga dingga*) sound. This sound has playful connotations and, accompanying the anxiety-inducing content of the speech bubble, makes the anxiety cell's speech all the more of an irritant. This is difficult to translate, again, not only because many languages lack an ideophonic system as fully developed as that of Korean, but also because (like 힉 above) a closer transliteration of this sound (the "ding" adopted in many of the translations shown in Figure 4.10) already has an established meaning in many languages – the sound a bell makes when struck. The use of this onomatopoeia is therefore somewhat perplexing to readers of the English translation. Note how the Japanese fan translation (top right) gets past this by using ぷらぷら *(purapura)*, a more playful version of the phenomime for wandering aimlessly, ふらふら *(furafura)*. This is an example of how Japan's larger vocabulary of mimetic words makes it easier to find an equivalent that is both acceptable to the target readership, and adequate to the source text.

Figure 4.10 Anxiety cell makes Yumi worry about her clothes (clockwise from top-left: Korean original, Japanese fan translation, French fan translation, Italian fan translation, English official translation) in *Yumi's Cells*

Source: Lee 2015–20.

March Comes in Like a Lion, *Ep. 1, 16:51–18:25*

Another example comes in the first episode of *March Comes in Like a Lion,* in which the protagonist Kiriyama is suffering from depression, and has been invited to the house of some new friends: three sisters, who are living together with their grandfather in the aftermath of their mother's death. Kiriyama, who is exhausted and a bit malnourished from over-preparing for his last chess match, has collapsed asleep in their living room after the meal.

The scene begins with Kiriyama waking up and consists mostly of the middle sister rushing around because she is late for school, though these events are of little importance. What is more important is the idea that this household is a lively, happy, light-hearted, and a welcoming place that makes Kiriyama come out of his shell – the scene's importance lies in its emotional content. Bright visual effects, exaggerated movements, fast cutting, and on-screen ideophones are all used to convey this atmosphere. The abundance of elements that come together to give the sense of this happy home create a certain level of redundancy, meaning that the loss of the occasional element (such as an ideophone here or there) does not damage the overall idea to a great extent.

As with the earlier examples, simply leaving the onomatopoeia untranslated allows the visual elements of the comic or the animation to take over. That being said, any meaning that is contained within in an ideophone alone is awkward in English and generally hard to compensate for with an English word. The official subtitles avoid providing any translations at all for the ideophones. The fansub, however, does involve attempts to overtly translate some of them, resorting to a mix of verbs, adverbs, and English onomatopoeia; meanwhile the official dub not only gives subtitles for all the onomatopoeia but also re-records them with their English equivalent. A comparison of translated and untranslated elements is shown in Table 4.1.

Table 4.1 A comparison of translated and untranslated elements in *March Comes in Like a Lion*, Ep. 1, 16:51–18:25

Original background element	Use/context	Fansub	Official sub	Official dub
じ｢	Sound for a fixed gaze	STARE (in subtitles)	N/A	N/A
びゅん	Sound for thrusting something out in a hurry	N/A	N/A	N/A
きっぱり	Sound for a mother-figure who has got up early in the morning for work and wakes her child, who will fall back to sleep (it's her own fault)	Blunt (in subtitles)	N/A	"Straightforward" (spoken in high-pitched voice)
ばば｢ん！！	Sound of a long sausage being thrust at the protagonist for his lunch	BA-BAAAM (in subtitles)	N/A	"Baa-Baan" (spoken in high-pitched voice)
はっし	Sound of grasping the sausage quickly and firmly	GRASP (in subtitles)	N/A	"Hasshi" (spoken in high-pitched voice)

(*continued*)

Table 4.1 Cont.

Original background element	Use/context	Fansub	Official sub	Official dub
ええっっ！？	Interjection of protagonist when he is surprised and uncertain about being left alone in the sister's house	Ehhh?! (in subtitles)	N/A	N/A
ビシイイッッ	Sound of a thumbs-up with very positive emotion	BAAAAM (in subtitles)	N/A	"Baa-Baan" (spoken in high pitched voice)
ガ┌ンン	Sound of protagonist's surprise at being given the house keys	GONG (in subtitles)	N/A	"Gaaaa" (spoken in high pitched voice)
シ┌ン...	Sound of protagonist left alone in the house with keys after the sister leaves for school	SILENCE (in subtitles)	N/A	SILENCE (in subtitles)

4.2.6 Culturally Specific Objects and Activities

Translation of references (overt or implied) to culturally specific objects and activities poses particular difficulties that have less to do with emotion and more to do with complex intertextuality. It can be very difficult to compensate in translation for the accretion of a vast body of shared experience and knowledge that may be assumed in the source language; in other words, meaning that is created very efficiently in the source language can be extremely burdensome to reproduce in the target language.

Nichijou, Ep. 6, 6:13–7:01

One example in *Nichijou* involves the combination of body language and culturally specific terms, which make the translation difficult. In the scene, the go-soccer club is having a meeting with only two members present. Having nothing to do (go-soccer is not a real game), the head of the club asks his partner, who is reading, to play a game of *isseno* with him. He starts to play, shouting out "two" while sticking out one of his fingers, but he soon complains that she is not joining in the game. The camera cuts then to her one finger sticking out subtly from the hand holding her book. The president smiles, and the skit ends.

As you can tell from this description, the skit is hard to understand without knowing what *isseno* means. *Isseno* is a game that roughly involves one person in a group, the guesser, saying "*isseno*" and then a number, everyone else in the group sticks out however many fingers at the same time the guesser speaks. If the guesser's number matches with how many fingers are stuck out then they get to leave the game, and the last person left is the loser.

Knowing the rules is integral to the narrative of the skit because you need to know that the other member sticking out a finger shows that she is participating in the game, and that the fact that she stuck out a single finger means the game is already over (the president guessed correctly there were two fingers). Hence the skit can end with the game ending. As should be clear from this description, there is no way to pack all of that information on the term *isseho* into the subtitles and, even if there were, the skit might be over by the time the audience had read it.

Nichijou, *Ep. 6, 2:16–6:10*

Nichijou provides another illustrative example. In this case, a game is being played between two characters that it is assumed the audience is aware of. The game is *shitori*, in which a player must take the last character of a word (as written in phonetic script, which could also be thought of in moraic terms) and use it as the first character of a new word. Words cannot be repeated and the player who uses a word ending in ん ("*n*") loses because no Japanese words start with this character.

The nature of this game adds a new level of difficulty to the translation. Not only must the translation deal with explaining the rules of the game but it must deal with the sound similarity that is integral to the playing of the game. For example, in this skit one of the characters must find a word beginning with う ("*u*") to respond with. In addition, they must draw a picture of what their chosen word is (this is a game of picture *shitori*, the rules of which are self-explanatory). The friend thinking decides upon a response as follows:

YUUKO: Let's see! U, huh? Okay.

JAPANESE ORIGINAL: さって、"う"ね…よし。 *("satte, 'u' ne… yoshi")*
 Yuuko then starts to draw and we cut to Mio receiving her picture and word

MIO: Uni. No, usa… It's a cow?!
JAPANESE ORIGINAL: うに、いや、うさ…うしかよ？！ *("uni, iya, usa… ushi ka yo?")*

The drawing of the cow is terrible, hence the joke. As you can see from this exchange the translation struggles to connect the word "cow" to its sound in Japanese, *ushi*. In order to understand that the picture is terrible we must understand that it is meant to be a cow but in order to understand the game we must understand that *ushi* starts with the sound *u*. Translation becomes even more complex with the introduction of katakana words later in the game.

The Live *(더라이브)*

This short example, shown in Figure 4.11, is from the fan translation of a manhwa called *The Live* (더라이브). In the manhwa, a character is insulting

Figure 4.11 One character insults another in *The Live*
Source: Ant Studio 2020.

another for still being childish and believing in fantasies. To do so they use a recent Korean neologism 중2병 *(jung-ee-byeong)* which could be parsed quite robotically as "middle school second grade disease." As a recent neologism, this doesn't have an easy equivalent in English. The term refers to middle school-aged students who are so obsessed with games and other popular fantasy media that they begin to think it is their reality.

The translator tries to get round this in quite a novel way, using a transliteration of a Japanese equivalent, *chuuni.* This means exactly the same thing, but the translator uses it on the assumption that the English reading fans of manhwa are more familiar with manga and might know what the term means (it is a term often kept romanised in translations).

This approach is reminiscent of what we sometimes see in subtitling. Most famously, perhaps, is in Bong Joon-ho's smash hit film *Parasite* (2019), in which subtitler Darcey Paquet invented a new term, "*ram-don,*" to refer to a Korean noodle dish called *jjapaguri.* The dish is a mixture of two different brands of Korean instant noodles (*jjapaghetti* and *neguri*), hence its name. However, Paquet renamed the dish, using a word partially made from Japanese morphemes (-*don* comes from the Japanese *udon*, while *ram-* is taken from the Korean *ramyeon*, though some viewers may mistakenly assume it is from the Japanese *ramen*). This choice was made on the basis that Japanese udon noodles will be widely known, which will aid viewers' comprehension.

4.2.7 Puns and Wordplay

Puns are often instrumental in comics and graphic fiction. The audience's understanding of the pun cannot be easily compensated for, and, unlike facial expressions, ideophones, or interjections, do not play a key role in expressing emotion but are rather a centrepiece in the scene: the joke. This means that any confusion in the translation can lead to confusion for the reader/viewer. This difficulty led to the use of translator's notes in all of the examples described in this section.

These examples are taken from the first five episodes of *Yakitate!! Japan* (焼きたて!!ジャぱん). The puns involved are difficult to handle in subtitles because they require explanation of the Japanese sounds for the wordplay to make any sense. Even the title of the show presents difficulty for translators. The source language title is written with the element corresponding to "Japan" written as ジャぱん. The change from katakana to hiragana mid-word emphasises the separation of the two sounds – Ja-pan – making the audience think of the split Ja-pan rather than just the English name for 日本. With that sound in mind and the start of the tittle 焼きたて *(yaki tate;* "freshly baked") the pun is obvious – the pan of Ja-pan working with the Japanese word for bread ぱん *(pan).* This is a pun that is used throughout the series, given that it is the protagonist's dream to make a bread that is unique to Japanese cuisine – which he wants to call the ジャぱん ("Ja Pan").

Yakitate!! Japan, *Ep. 1, 16:45*

Here the protagonist is trying to make his Japanese bread (the eponymous Ja
pan) that can go with fermented soybeans (納豆、*nattō*) for breakfast. Upon
eating the bread, the grandfather exclaims that he approves of the bread
(approve = 納得、*nattoku*), leading to a pun on the similarity of *nattō* and
nattoku.

Yakitate!! Japan, *Ep. 1, 16:52*

In the same scene, the grandfather goes on to exclaim, "*kaminomizoshiru*,"
because of how well the bread combines with another staple of Japanese
cuisine, miso soup. Two alternate ways of writing this exclamation then
appear in the background revealing two different potential meanings of the
statement in Japanese:

> 神のみぞ知る ("only god knows/only the gods know (the divine truth)")
> and 神のみぞ汁 ("the miso soup of the gods").
>
> (Yakitate!! Japan, Ep. 2, 19:00)

In this scene the protagonist, who is often played as an idiot for the audience's
amusement, does not think that curry comes from India. When the other
characters try to correct him by pointing out that the word curry is a foreign katakana word from India, the protagonist disagrees, arguing that the
Japanese word for curry (カレー, *karē*) comes from the Japanese word spicy
(辛い, *karai*, which when pronounced in the rural drawl of the protagonist
becomes →辛えー *karee*).

Yakitate!! Japan, *Ep. 2, 22:08 and Ep. 3, 13:45*

Two puns in this scene revolve around the word croissant (クロワッサン,
kurowassan). In the first, the idiotic protagonist, who doesn't know any French
baking, is asked to make a croissant, only to ask who Mr Kurowa (クロワさ
ん) is and where he can be found. The protagonist even goes as far as to call
his sister to ask who Mr Kurowa is, much to her bewilderment. In the second
pun one of the character's croissants comes out of the oven incredibly burnt.
This leads the judge to exclaim that it's not just a croissant (クロワッサン,
kurowassan) but a black-croissant (黒ワッサン, *kurowassan*). The translator
opted for translator's notes to explain both the misinterpretation of croissant
as Mr Kurowa, and how the Japanese word for black (黒い、*kuroi*) can also
play into the word croissant.

Yakitate!! Japan, *Ep. 4, 16:05*

This is the first of a group of puns throughout the series that play on the word
うまい *(umai)* which means "delicious." In this case a plot point is contrived

such that the manager of the bakery wants the characters to make bread good enough that a horse would eat it. His contention is that breads with too much butter, eggs, and milk that are hard for people with allergens get ignored by a horse's discerning palette. When asking the characters to make their bread, the manager says it must be a bread good for a horse (馬いいパン, *uma-ii-pan*), in other words delicious bread (馬味いパン, *umai-pan*). As you can see the pun between "delicious" and "good for a horse" is reinforced by having the script used to spell delicious include the kanji for horse.

Yakitate!! Japan, Ep. 4, 11:58

In this scene, a horse is shown chomping down on a piece of bread that it likes. The sound effect that flashes up on the screen is "chomp" (バク, *baku*); however, it is spelt with the kanji characters for horse (馬) and eat (食) and thus appears as "馬食," playing with the fact that it is a horse that is eating.

Yakitate!! Japan, Ep. 5, 19:18

In another pun using the word "delicious" (うまい, *umai*), the protagonist tries to make allergen-free bread by using goat's milk instead of cow's milk. He is successful and so the manager proclaims that the bread is a delicious bread (うめーパン, *umē-pan*). Here the wordplay is that pronouncing *umai* as *umē* (which can indicate a rural, male, or young speaker) makes the word associable with the onomatopoeia for the sound a goat makes, "め" *(mē)*, making a pun about the protagonist's use of goat's milk in the bread.

4.2.8 Under-translation

Previous examples have demonstrated that often there is a need for what might be thought of as over-translation (extra efforts being made to compensate for particular difficulties). However, studies show different interpretations of eye contact, touching, and conversational responsiveness across languages, and that the tendency has been for under-translation. This section will look at under-translation, typically where physical gestures that require a certain level of cultural knowledge for comprehension are left without any additional explanation. That these examples involve physical gestures or visual elements unaccompanied by text (or speech) in the source may reflect a greater readiness, or sense of obligation, to more fully explain translation of text. That is to say, when presented with dialogue or written text, the translator feels compelled to provide a translation (viewers will generally wonder why speech has not been translated, and be critical of a strategy of omission), and the natural desire to create a translation that is fully understood leads the translator to provide extra explanations where seemingly necessary to comprehension. When, on the other hand, the meaning in question is created through a physical gesture, there is less motivation for a translator to consider the sign as within the scope of their task. The result is that – although the translator may quite reasonably take the view that a (sighted) viewer can see the physical gesture as well as them without any need for mediation – the meanings immediately apparent to source-culture viewers will often remain opaque to viewers from other cultures.

Nichijou, Ep. 1, 8:26–8:45

In the skit shown in Figure 4.12, Mai, a principal character in *Nichijou*, and her dog are in a park. Mai throws a frisbee for her dog and the dog runs and leaps into the air, only for the frisbee to explode in mid-air; the camera cuts to Mai holding a smoking rifle. She makes a V sign with her fingers and the skit ends.

The underlying absurd joke of the skit is clearly understandable to an English audience: what initially looks like a game of catch with the dog quickly turns out to be clay pigeon shooting, to the surprise of the dog as well as the audience. It is the added punchline of the V symbol that may be difficult to for English-language viewers to understand. Japanese youth commonly use the V symbol (*pīsu sain*, ピースサイン) when posing for photos to show a sense of happiness, fun, and celebration. This relates to its meaning as a shorthand for

Figure 4.12 Mai makes a peace sign in *Nichijou*
Source: Ishihara 2011.

"victory," which is the sense in which it is used here. Mai's celebration adds emphasis to the sudden change of goals; we and the dog thought this was a game of catch, meanwhile Mai is celebrating her clay pigeon shooting ability.

This is difficult to translate to an English audience as the V sign (with palm facing away from the gesturer), though having a link to the idea of victory as it was used during the Second World War, is seen as old-fashioned and bearing more serious political associations to peace than associations to casual celebration (Morris, 1979: 226–40). In the anime the subtitles do not try to translate the symbol. It should be noted however that to those interested in Japanese culture, particularly "Cool Japan" culture as it exists on the Internet, the V sign is easily understandable.

Nichijou, *Ep. 11, 16:10–16:30*

Throughout *Nichijou*, the audience follows the attempts of the go-soccer club to gather new members, despite go-soccer (囲碁サッカー) not being a real sport. An earlier skit in episode 11 has told the audience that the head of the go-soccer club, Daiku, is in fact a wealthy heir to Daiku Industries. In the earlier skit, Daiku promises to pay a friend back for a favour by getting the friend some apple juice. He is then shown leaving school in a helicopter, telling his chauffeur that they will need to buy a blender and an apple orchard on the way back (a ludicrous way of giving a friend some apple juice). The skit we are discussing occurs later in the episode with a return to the go-soccer club's efforts to get new members. Sekiguchi, the only other club member, is standing stunned in front of the school. The camera then cuts to two large banners hung in front of the school. They read:

> Aiming at number one in Japan (めざせ日本一, *mezase nippon'ichi*)
> congratulations to the Go-Soccer club for getting to the prefectural competition" (祝 囲碁サッカー部 県大「出場, *shuku igo sakkā-bu ken taikai shutsujō*).

The audience understands this as another ploy to improve the image of the club and get new members. Sekiguchi, still stunned, turns to Daiku at her side who is making the symbol shown in Figure 4.13 (palm facing upwards, with the tips of forefinger and thumb touching and the remaining three fingers extended outwards).

The skit then ends with a cut to the friend from earlier, to whom Daiku said he would give the juice. The friend, now holding his new blender and his freshly blended apple juice (Figure 4.14), says, This must be the power of Daiku Industries" (これがダイク財閥の力か！, *kore ga daiku zaibatsu no chikara ka!*). The joke about Daiku's wealth is worked in as a reference to the earlier skit involving the apple juice.

The difficulty here comes with the fact that an Anglo-American audience may not understand that the pinching of the thumb and the forefinger is a

Figure 4.13 Daiku shocks his clubmate with his wealth in *Nichijou*
Source: Ishihara 2011.

Figure 4.14 Daiku's friend is amazed at Daiku's wealth in *Nichijou*
Source: Ishihara 2011.

symbol for money. This will leave them none the wiser as to Daiku's response to his friend's stunned silence, in which he is non-verbally expressing something like: "I got the banners up there through money. I am very rich, and money is how we will win people to the club." Misunderstanding this hand gesture also makes it harder for the audience to link Daiku and Sekiguchi's interaction to the friend with the blender and the apple juice.

Nichijou, *Ep. 1, 15:20–15:50*

In the skit shown in Figure 4.15, one of the main characters, Mio, is having a ridiculous fantasy about a boy on whom she has a crush, in which he rides up to her on a goat and proposes to her. The camera then cuts to her collapsing from a nosebleed. The joke here is that this fantasy, which appears ridiculous, was attractive enough to Mio that she fainted from a nosebleed. The link between arousal and nosebleeds, a common trope of anime and manga, is not established in Anglo-American culture. Without some additional form of explanation, this connection may be confusing. but explaining what is happening would ruin the pacing of the joke.

In the three examples from *Nichijou* that have been described, the translator has not opted to add any kind translator's notes, risking the loss of those meanings created by the various physical gestures. The pacing inherent in the

Figure 4.15 Yuuko faints from a nosebleed in *Nichijou*
Source: Ishihara 2011.

TL/N: IN JAPAN, SENIOR GUYS WILL USUALLY GIVE THEIR SECOND JACKET BUTTON TO A GIRL THEY CARE ABOUT.

Figure 4.16 A senpai tries to give his button away at graduation (English fan translation) in *Kaguya-sama: Love is War*, chapter 202

Source: Akasaka 2016.

format (these animations are, of course, moving images) mean that lengthy explanatory text will either be impossible to read, or require changes be made to the underlying video's speed, both of which are factors that will contribute to a decision against such a strategy. Where there is no verbal language, more traditionally seen as the object of translation, such factors are more likely to be decisive.

There are, nonetheless, cases when non-verbal expressions do not go entirely unexplained. The barriers to such paratextual material are lower in written texts than video, as the pacing is less set in stone and additional text can often be inserted for the reader to take in at their leisure. In an example taken from *Kaguya-sama: Love is War* (Figure 4.16), a senior can be seen giving his button to a junior from his cheer club (there is a Japanese tradition that usually involves a graduate giving their button to a girl they like). The character's dialogue refers to his body language and the translator uses a translator's note to explain his body language.

4.2.9 Formatting and Graphic Narratives

Graphic materials present a unique problem for translators. Firstly, they require graphic skills, which translators often lack. Secondly, they often require reformatting to accommodate the new text, with issues such as reading direction and text volume to contend with. Manga and manhua are read from right to left and from top to bottom. Manhwa, however, are read

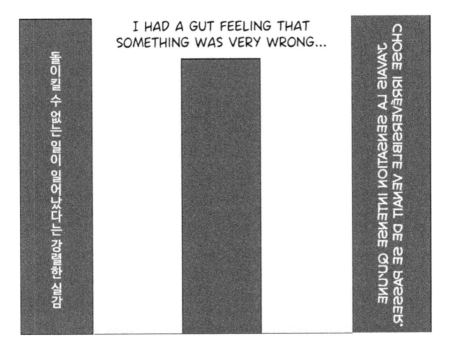

Figure 4.17 A character finds out about a friend's tragic accident (Korean original, left; English, middle; French, right) in *The Boxer*

Source: Ji-Hoon 2019.

from left to right and from top to bottom. Webtoons are read from top to bottom, allowing for infinite scrolling. This can be used strategically to depict the movement of objects in the artwork, or the passage of time. Changes in language often mean changes in reading direction, which can subsequently result in awkwardness, the loss of intended effects, or the removal of tone or emotion (also relevant to "emotional equivalence").

Webtoons are read by scrolling downwards rather than by page, and Korean webtoons will sometimes exploit this by stretching words downward. Figure 4.17 shows an example this, in *The Boxer*, Episode 41. Here, a character learns of a close friend's fatal accident, and her looming sense of dread appears on the static background of a TV screen, emphasising the incomprehensibility of the tragedy. English and French, both of which are read from left to right, are two languages that present difficulties to the translator here. The English translator has opted for readability but loses the possible thematic importance of the words layering over the static, as well as making the static itself appear out of place. The French translator has opted to retain the layout, resulting in a reading experience that is somewhat awkward.

4.3 Korean Popular Culture Fan Translation

The Korea Foundation has estimated the number Korean popular culture fans at around 89 million people across 113 countries (Elfving-Hwang 2019), though some researchers propose that "the number in social media seems to be even greater" (Kiaer and Kim 2021). Indeed, social media has played an instrumental role in the growth of fandom and the phasal development of the Korean Wave (Jin 2016), and so defines the stage in which *Hallyu* moved from sub-cultural to global phenomenon. Importantly, it isn't the official accounts of artists or agencies online that have orchestrated the growth in the influential K-fan community, but the fans themselves. Their participation has been so successful, in fact, that it has led to a growing culture of high-culture engagement from an initially low-culture interest. Evidence can be seen in the twenty-six Korean words recently added to the *Oxford English Dictionary*.

Due to K-fandoms being incredibly international and cross-cultural, fan translators form a truly integral part of the community. The fact that Twitter is a platform that values and pushes content that is current and relevant can pose a problem for an international fandom when the most current content is in a language that the majority of the fandom does not fully understand. Thus, fan translators work as a bridge between the new Korean content and the overseas fans, who want to consume that content as quickly (and accurately) as possible.

4.3.1 BTS Fandom and Translation on Twitter

A glimpse at some of the most prominent translators in the BTS fandom on Twitter shows them to have an immense reach on the platform. Many popular translation accounts have several hundred thousand, or even over one million, followers and are among the most popular accounts in the BTS fan community.

Although fan-translation of Korean content online is by no means a new phenomenon, these communities and the discussions we can observe online are much more evolved than they used to be. Earlier international K-pop fans were lucky if they could find blogs offering translations of lyrics or dramas online, and those that were available were not suitable for the more dynamic discussions of the content that we see today. Now that the online K-pop community is mainly active on Twitter, open discussions of the content and translations of the content are much easier to achieve. Now that people are more easily connected and united in online communities based on their interests, more content can also be circulated in these communities. To summarise, the K-pop space on Twitter has grown to the size it is now because of an ever-growing number of international fans/consumers of content, as well as the many fan contributors.

Fan-contributors in themselves are an interesting phenomenon. Akin to how fan artists spend hours painting their favourite idols and uploading their art to engage with other fans, fan-translators put in a lot of effort to consistently translate new information and content for the rest of the fans in their community. Many fan-translators are not professional translators but rather amateurs using their language skills to perform a free service for the rest of their community, and a labor intensive one at that – many translate not only song lyrics and new official updates, but even idols' live broadcasts on different media.

Many of those who are not a part of these communities may question why fans would want to participate in such an arduous task. To answer this, it is important to first understand how these accounts work. Fan-translation accounts are not exclusive to the BTS fandom or even the K-pop community, but often play an important role in any international fandom in which translated textual updates concerning the original content adds to the fans' experience of that content. It's also widespread in the manga and anime communities, which have also grown immensely on Twitter. However, the K-pop community is particularly reliant on translations, judging from a consideration of the sheer volume of content that is put out – if you follow a K-pop group with several members, not only will their agency post updates on what they are doing, but the individual members may post updates online too, or even do live broadcasts that are hard for international fans to follow without subtitles or commentary. One could argue that this is also a big part of why K-pop has grown to become such an international phenomenon – there's simply so much content to dive into. It must then also be considered that such content would not have been as accessible were it not for the many fan-translators. While a music video can often be enjoyed without understanding the lyrics to the song, the language barrier becomes much more apparent when fans want to enjoy the other content from their idols (interviews, variety shows, or even movies or other media they've starred in). Accordingly, it's no wonder that the BTS fan-translations on Twitter have such a large following. Fans follow them for what are often daily updates.

The example in Figure 4.18 shows a translation of a Weverse post, where BTS member Jin is interacting with a fan's post. The translators usually put the date at the top in the Korean order (YYMMDD), attach an image of the original post, and use emojis or other identifiers to show who's speaking in their translation. In many K-pop fandoms, each member will usually have an animal that they're associated with – we can see that the member Jin is depicted here as a hamster. The number listed below the tweet shows the level of engagement the tweet has had in the eight hours it has been up. With almost 5,000 likes on the translation of a very simple comment, it's not hard to see the type of influence that fan-translators could potentially have.

One fan translator, with over 200,000 followers, showed how she does her translations of live broadcasts in a video on Twitter (Figure 4.19). In the video, she shows the set-up she uses. She listens to the broadcast from one device and then types her simultaneous interpretations out on Twitter on her computer. Here she also shows how the animal emojis representing each

Figure 4.18 Translation of Weverse post and comment by a fan translator

member are used as a type of shortcut for translators, so that they don't have to type out the full names each time. She then goes on to describe the process of "live translating" (simultaneous interpretation) and how she must be able to perform several tasks at once. The first is listening to and understanding the Korean, the second is translating the Korean to English in her mind, and the third is "speed-typing" the translations into tweets. Finally, she notes that she must do these three tasks while continuously taking a broader view, based on the ongoing conversation, as to what to translate and how. She cites this as the reason why it is impossible for translators to catch everything; they must prioritise the sentences and exchanges they can hear clearly and that are most important to the overall context. Finally, she shows how enjoyable she finds the experience.

This post provides a glimpse into the methods and thought process that underlie the work of amateur fandom translators. It shows that despite a lack of formal training in translation, they are able to identify the different processes required, and how the demands of these processes affect the final product. Amateur translators, like Sora, can even be a source of information for large followings, as was demonstrated in the tweet of the video showing Sora's translation process, which has 35,000 likes; providing education on translation to a much wider audience than would otherwise be possible, who may then also begin taking part in translation within the community.

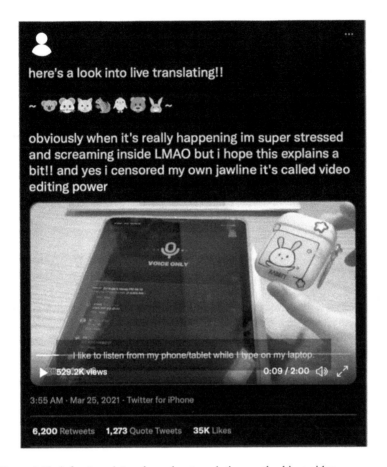

Figure 4.19 A fan translator shows her translation method in a video

4.3.2 *Fans Join Mainstream Conversations about Translation*

Through platforms like Twitter, fandoms are now a part of wider conversations around what translation should be. They're able to interact directly with the translator and criticise their translations. This has not been possible with more traditional forms of media, such as books or articles.

Readers are not passive consumers, and Twitter even encourages discussion through replies and quote retweets; functions that are used widely in Korean fandom communities. One of the smaller translation accounts, referred to here as Translator A experienced this grass-roots criticism for their translation of a live broadcast. Some fans were unhappy that the translator chose to convey the atmosphere and feeling between the members, in addition to what was being said, by commenting on the meaning of the non-verbal

(a)

(b)

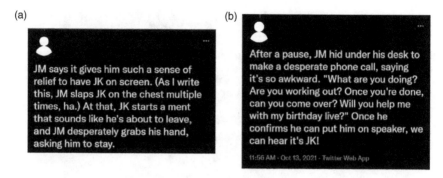

Figure 4.20 Fan translations from Translator A of the live broadcast on Jimin's birthday, 13 October 2021

Figure 4.21 A supporter shows their appreciation for Translator A's translations

communication between them as well. Some fans criticised her for subjective characterisation of the members, arguing that these characterisations could be used to criticise the members (Figure 4.20).

While translator's notes are frequent when translating from Korean to English (examples from manhwa have been treated above), Translator A goes beyond that, removing the author's notes from the parentheses and incorporating them in their final product, which gives the reader a different experience of the content being translated. Much of this description is of the members' non-verbal expression, achieved through Translator A's use of certain adverbs (e.g., "desperately") and attributes intentions to the members with intentions (e.g., "sounds like he's about to leave"). Although Translator A's tweets contain translations, they also feature Translator A's own interpretation of the situation, which is not necessarily representative of the actual intent behind the members' actions. The question is then whether such an approach is reliable for those wanting accurate translations, although some of her supporters even made the point that translation is inherently more than just a mechanical, word-for-word process, and always requires interpretation of multiple factors (Figure 4.21).

Figure 4.22 An Army member's response to Translator A's apology

Figure 4.23 An Army member's response to Translator A's apology

Translator A apologised, explaining that they use adverbs to portray not just the language but also the mood between the members. They stated that they do take on criticism, reviewed their live tweets, and aimed to do better. Translator A's critics, however, were not satisfied with the apology (see Figures 4.22 and 4.23). While Translator A's supporters underlined that the work is undertaken for free and as such should not be criticised so harshly, the critics argued that there is a serious responsibility that comes with a large following. If people are misinformed by such content, the criticism can come back to the members (in this case BTS's Jimin). The Army (this term is used to refer to BTS's fanbase) take this responsibility very seriously, not wanting to reflect negatively on the members that they respect and look up to.

Translator A's case exhibits some of the most common and relevant issues in translation, proving that fan translation is not exempt from the scrutiny and debate of the more traditional facets of translation, despite its fundamentally amateur nature (although perhaps non-pecuniary rewards such as status within the community need to be considered). This issues include the argument as to whether faithfulness or localisation are more appropriate, or ethical, and whether the translator should be considered a co-author for the creativity that is a vital part of the practice.

4.3.3 Fan Armies, Translation, and the Korean Media

The influence of fan translators has even been recognised in Korea. In a political talk show called *Kim Eo-jun's Daseuboeida* (김어준의 다스뵈이다) on YouTube, music critic Kim Young-dae was invited to talk about the influence of fan Army translators. The host, Kim Eo-jun, starts the segment by explaining how he and his team had noticed a large number of English comments on one of his videos where he'd mentioned BTS. He was confused, as the show doesn't have subtitles. The comments mentioned the music critic Kim Young-dae, as well as criticising the Korean media and their reaction to BTS' Grammy nomination. Eventually the host found out that an Army translator (referred to here as Translator B) had translated a short clip from the show and uploaded it to her Twitter as a preview of a full translation. Army members had then found the video on YouTube and commented directly on it. Kim Eo-jun mentions how he then realised how the Army must have sympathised with the argument he was making in that segment, which is why it was ideal for translation. The video goes on to credit Translator B for the English subtitles of the BTS segment in the video.

The original segment of this podcast that drew attention from the Army was focused on how the Korean media understates or underestimates BTS' accomplishments. They talked about why it is that Korean media don't discuss BTS as much as one might expect, and under-report their new records or other relevant news. Kim Eo-jun describes it as a "cultural lag," where the domestic media is not capable of keeping up with the rate of BTS' growth in popularity, and as such they end up hesitating to comment. He stresses how some older reporters may think back to their youth when they reported on events in an overly nationalist way,[2] and how that may be part of what's holding them back. He also makes the point that the industry in Korea may be ignoring or downplaying BTS' success because BTS as a phenomenon exists outside their sphere of influence, and the band does not depend on them for success. As such, it's not in their interest to acknowledge BTS' success. BTS doesn't depend on domestic or international promotion, and should a journalist try to criticise the group or any of its members, there is a massive fanbase ready to launch a counter-offensive. Thus, it's easier and safer for the journalists to downplay BTS' success.

He also comments on how some people frame BTS as being supporters of Moon Jae-in and then purposefully attack them for political reasons. In conclusion, he argues that it is a combination of all these issues that is to blame for how the domestic press treats BTS. Kim Young-dae proceeds to explain what translation accounts are and how they operate. As a music critic who has written about BTS for years, Kim Young-dae is extremely well informed and aware of this phenomenon, and he explains it to the host in great detail. He's especially impressed by the speed, quality, and diversity of the fan-translators' work. He underlines the fact that the translators not only provide textual translations, but also cultural context so that foreigners are able to understand the content on a deeper level. Considering his body of work on BTS, Kim Yong-dae describes himself as quite well-known among foreign Armies. You can even see this in the comments on the video (Figure 4.24), where Army members mention how Young-dae "calls out" the Korean press for treating BTS unfairly. This is something Young-dae directly addresses as well; he's seen how Armies have talked about BTS, and their fandom being treated unfairly in the media (also outside of Korea), but whenever they try to bring this up seriously, people accuse them of being crazy fangirls. That's why it's so important for them to see it discussed in a more serious forum by Koreans.

The relationship between the press and the Armies is complex, and an integral reason for why the fandom includes so many content-creators (or contributors) such as translators. It seems as if the disregard for BTS, their fandom, and their countless successes from the traditional Korean media has produced a gap in content that the Armies have stepped in to fill. This affects the domestic Army too, so it is not only an international matter either. When the press does not report on or translate content surrounding BTS, fan-translators step up and provide content for their fellow fans. This sentiment is prevalent in the comment shown in Figure 4.25, in which a fan is echoing the sentiment Kim Young-dae. The commenter expresses how grateful they are to be taken seriously as an Army, as they feel Armies are often labelled as screaming youths, ignoring that many fans are adults with buying power and

Figure 4.24 A Comment on Kim Eo-jun's *DasVweda*, praising Kim Young-dae for sticking up for BTS and their Armies

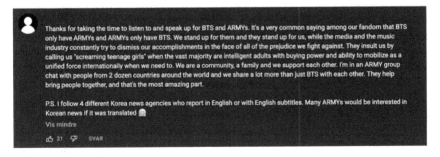

Figure 4.25 A Comment on Kim Eo-jun's *DasVweda* expressing frustration with how the press treats the fandom in a patronising manner, as well as expressing desire to consume more translated Korean news

the "ability to mobilize as a unified force internationally." This comment in particular shows how aware Army members are of their power.

An interesting example of fan-contributors (including translators) coming together to provide comprehensive analysis of certain situations pertaining to BTS is the White Paper Project. It came about in late 2018, after images of member Jimin wearing a controversial shirt began to circulate online that same year. The paper also covers other "incidents" from BTS' past, such as other controversial clothing and photoshoots in historically sensitive places. The editors-in-chief are two well-known BTS translators from Twitter, and the entire paper is written with the help of twenty writers and four translators. It's a project of great magnitude, spanning over 100 pages of writing produced by non-paid fan-contributors. The paper is available in both English and Korean and gives an overview of the events that sparked controversy at the time, while going on to explain the historical context and response from fandom. Although this paper does not represent the views of the Army fanbase as a whole, it does demonstrate how the fandom mobilises, collaboratively, and utilises translation to support their idols.

4.3.4 A Popular Topic of the 2020s

Translation has, in fact, been a popular topic of mainstream news recently (Rosenblatt 2021), again stimulated by Korean popular culture – this time, by the Korean Netflix television show *Squid Game* (2021). Online debate was sparked by Young-mi Mayer's viral TikTok post criticising the English subtitles of the show. One viewer, referred to here as Critic X, criticised Netflix for having subtitles that she claimed would result in Korean- and English-speakers "watching a different show." One example she provided was of the English translation of *"oppa"* as "old man," along with other lines she felt were important to the characterisation of the characters and even to grasping the main point of certain episodes.

Young-mi's claims were investigated and discussed by fellow fans, who then posted their findings and thoughts. This provides a typical representative example of how Korean popular culture translators participate in educating other fans. An occasional BTS translator on Twitter, referred to here as Translator C, retweeted the video with her criticism of the original creator's opinions. Translator C pointed out that the viral TikTok had not used the English subtitles as an example, but the English closed captions. The closed captions are not translations of the character's Korean lines, but rather transcriptions of the English dub. Closed captions are often used by the deaf or hard-of-hearing, as they not only are transcriptions of the English dub but include descriptions of the other sounds in the media. Figure 4.26 shows Translator C's post, in which they show how the subtitles differ from the closed captions.

Translator C specifically uses the character Minyeo's line as an example. She shows how Minyeo's original line *"mwol bwa?"* (뭘 봐?) was changed to

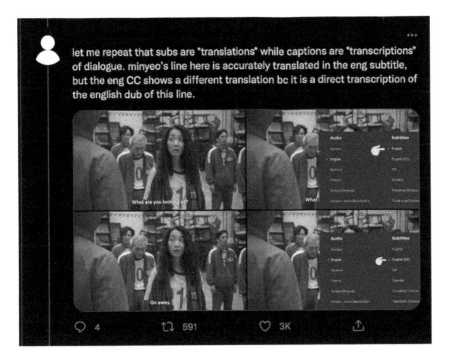

Figure 4.26 Translator C compares the English subtitles and closed captions for *Squid Game* on Netflix

"Go away" in the English dub, to match the mouth movements of the actor. However, the English subtitles express meaning that is more like the original, with the subtitle reading "What are you looking at?" Translator C argues that it is misguided to direct this kind of frustration about the translation at the closed captions. Restrictions associated with the convention to match dubbing as closely as possible to the mouth movements of the characters are commonly accepted as resulting in sacrifices when it comes to meanings in the source dialogue. Translator C also commented on another scene with Minyeo, where she uses the honorific *oppa* (오빠). Honorifics are often debated when it comes to the translation of Korean, since English tends to lack satisfactory equivalents. They also mean different things in different situations, which Translator C points out in the tweet in Figure 4.27. If one looks up the definition, "older brother" may be the first result in a dictionary, but it can also be used to address a woman's romantic partner. Translator C argues that the word "babe," which appears in the English subtitles (instead of "old man," which appears in the closed captions), is appropriate in the context. On this occasion, the address term shows Minyeo is trying to appeal to Deoksu by reminding him of their sexual relationship, rather than expressing her juniority, or teasing him for being older.

Figure 4.27 Translator C comments on the translation of the word *oppa* in *Squid Game*

Translator C's thread responding to criticism of the perceived translations in *Squid Game* demonstrates again the communal aspect of fan translation – their sense of shared responsibility and constant exchange of discourse. It also shows the power to educate that comes with this democratic approach to translation. Those with greater knowledge are able to teach less experienced consumers how to make judgements about the accuracy and quality of translations. This then contributes to an improved linguistic understanding of what translation is among people without formal training in the field.

Fan translators like Translator C play an important role online, beyond influencing, as guides for the increasing numbers of fans who want to understand and even produce content for the popular culture with which they choose to engage. Moreover, fans appear to want to communicate with each other, debating, educating, and developing translations that meet the needs of the consumers but that have the interests of the products at heart. Fan translators are emotionally invested in the products that they are translating.

4.4 A New Age of Translation Culture

We are now entering a new age of translation, and it has been in the making for some time. The examples provided in this chapter are just the tip of the iceberg. Fan translation has been evolving into more than just a practicality for international fandom since the 1990s. Today, this collaborative, multifaceted practice is part of greater culture of informed consumerism, collective responsibility, and participation in popular culture that was once passively enjoyed. The practice allows fans to feel that they are collaborating with their idols and their favourite manga or manhwa creators, rather than merely reading or watching from what feels like a distance. There is solidarity created among translators, between translators and other fans, among fans who are able to enjoy content together in their own language, and between the idols and the fans. The translators are invested emotionally in the creation of quality work and the integrity of the idols whom their content is representing. This fosters an environment productive in critical analysis, regulation, education, and ultimately a democratic approach to translation that can be beneficial in sharing more diverse views than might otherwise become available.

Notes

1 It is also common for fan translations of manga to use the English translation because of the easy access to the English, and more translators knowing English than Japanese (Fabbretti 2017).
2 He uses the term *gukppong* (국뽕), which refers to overexaggerated nationalism.

5   Conclusion

In this book, we have sought to shed some light on issues arising in translation between English and Japanese, and English and Korean, as a result of the different way in which pragmatic matters such as interpersonal relations are encoded in these languages, and the different cultural expectations in these regions. Chapters 2 and 3 treated the case studies of translation of *Harry Potter and the Philosopher's Stone* and *The Hobbit, or There and Back Again* into Japanese and Korean, respectively. We looked at the treatment of second-person pronouns and terms of address, in particular, to show how the significantly greater level of complexity in Japanese and Korean generally leads translators to explicitly crystallise their interpretations of the interpersonal dynamics of the source texts in their translations. Even if these interpretations are justifiable, this inevitably narrows the range of available interpretations available to the reader. In Chapter 4, we looked at fan translations into English of Japanese and Korean media, observing many examples of meaning being lost when translating in this direction. We saw that fan translators often add notes to provide more information on certain points that they expect may warrant explanation, but that non-verbal gestures are easily passed over in silence, considered outside the scope of translation. While we hope that the case studies provided in this book have highlighted how Japanese and Korean overtly reflecting pragmatic factors such as interpersonal relationships to a greater extent than English can have an impact on translation, we acknowledge that we have only scratched the surface of this issue. We hope that others will be inclined to perform similar case studies with other texts, and other language pairs, and that pragmatics in translation will receive more attention more generally.

5.1 The Future of Translation

The exponential increase in linguistic traffic will surely continue, creating more interaction and increasing the pool of shared words. In the Sunflower Model (Kiaer 2018), which represents the growth in the number of English words that are both cross-cultural and translingual, we see how words with their roots in one language have since migrated to be adopted by other

DOI: 10.4324/9781003217466-5

languages, simultaneously creating commonality in the shared origins of such words and diversity in the way that the word takes on different meanings in its new homes.

In the Sunflower, the petals represent the diversity of lexical items in areas such as their origins, forms, and meanings; the central seed-bearing body, "the dark core," represents the body of lexical items shared in common with a group of languages. When a sunflower first begins to grow, the dark core area is relatively small. As the plant grows, however, the sunflower head develops more seeds and expands. As the dark core of the flower gets bigger, the number of petals increases as well. In the model, the symbolic meaning of the centre of the plant where the seeds are formed represents the potential of, or the foundation of the birth of new translingual words that are born of several languages. The model reflects the production of the multiple "shared words" and new words, which develop in unpredictable directions as a result of the lexical interactions between speakers of different languages.

This model can, alternatively, be understood as a model for a specific repertoire of vocabulary. For example, a word of Korean origin, such as *oppa*, used to solely belong to Korea but is rapidly coming to be used by a global community as result of the popularity of the Korean wave. Another example can be from what we perhaps at one time might have preferred to refer to as "Asian Pasta": the most recognised word is instead noodle, a foreign import into English (which, interestingly, arrived from German). Nowadays, words such as *ramen*, *japchae*, and *udon* are becoming increasingly visible as terms referring to Japanese thin wheat noodles, Korean glass noodles, and Japanese thick wheat noodles respectively. Likewise, the Sunflower Model can vividly illustrate the simultaneous growth in both the commonalities and diversities of a global lexicon. As more and more exchanges occur cross-culturally, the number of words that are shared by multiple languages will increase, just as the increasing number of seeds in the centre of the sunflower cause it to expand. The proportion of words that are shared between people across the globe is exploding; nevertheless, lexical repertoires are also becoming increasingly diverse. That is to say, the size of the global lexicon is increasing but immeasurable diversity exists between the lexical repertoires of individuals.

The model also shows the almost immeasurable diversity of new English words which is the result of a rapid and dynamic lexical explosion. The birth of diversified English words and their expedited and simultaneous growth in unpredictable ways is accelerated by their multilingual individual lexical repertoire via the Internet, particularly through several channels of social media. When using the Internet, the lexical repertoire of individuals and communities spreads instantaneously across the globe, making it more difficult to accurately predict lexical behaviour based on the languages of one's parents. Kiaer (2018) argues that the notion of the nation-state, when applied to English language varieties such as in Korean English, Chinese English, and so on, does not in any way reflect the process of the creation of new translingual and transcultural words. General proficiency in English around the world at the moment is high, and is continuing to increase; the use of English as a lingua franca could mean, in one sense, that not everything will be translated between languages. That is to say, a wider pool of second-language English speakers can use that language to communicate among themselves and with first-language English speakers. On the other hand, however, the widening pool of shared words can also be seen as a growing collection of potential false friends. This is because of the different uses of words in their new homes. To return to an example we have already used in this chapter, the German *Nudel* does not have the same restriction to food of Asian origin as the word noodle has for many English speakers. Moreover, speakers from different backgrounds may want to transmit higher-level pragmatic issues, such as the pragmatics of interpersonal relationships, in a way that broader knowledge of certain lexical items from English is unlikely to prove helpful.

5.2 Big Data-Driven Machine Translation

As well as facilitating an explosion of interlingual and intercultural communication, which has played a role in the acceleration of shared words referred to above, the Internet has also allowed the collection of big data to fuel more powerful machine translation, and also provided easy public access to machine-translation platforms. The use of data-driven machine translation is becoming an ever-increasing part of our lives, and is playing a very useful role in bringing translation capabilities to every sector of life. AI systems and Google are collecting a lot of data from our activities online and using this to help bolster technology. This is extremely useful for diverse populations such as, for example, sections of the British public with diverse linguistic origins. The efficacy of machine translation has been growing exponentially alongside the volume of available data.

However, pragmatic issues of the kind discussed in this book remain difficult for data-driven machine translation. Translating English into appropriate natural Japanese or Korean requires an understanding of contextual factors at a level that may not be tagged in the relevant section of text itself, meaning that a copy-paste operation into a Google Translate window may be something of a dice roll when it comes to creating a target text that properly accounts for the interpersonal relations. Language often has situational meanings that cannot be retrieved from the data available to the machine-translation platform. This can be the hardest part of translation, and it makes it difficult to rely completely on the translating capabilities of technology. As we have discussed in this book, second-person pronouns, politeness levels, and speech styles do not follow an easily digestible (or, more importantly, definable) set of rules that could be provided to a machine. Solving these difficulties may require tagging texts in such a way as to account for pragmatic factors, or perhaps instructing machine-translation platforms to provide a set of alternative translations for the user to select based on an explanation of the pragmatic contexts that would make each alternative more likely to be suitable.

As such, pragmatic meanings are overtly reflected in languages like Japanese and Korean, this is an area that demands caution, and further attention, as machine-translation platforms continue to become more effective and more widely used.

5.3 The One-Inch Barrier and Translational Injustice

Parasite director Bong Joon-Ho, with filmmaker Sharon Choi acting as interpreter, encouraged American audiences to overcome the "one-inch-tall barrier of subtitles," which would give them access to the enjoyment of so many more amazing foreign films. Bong was clearly challenging the apparent aversion of American audiences to the marginal effort involved in reading subtitles, and expressing the view that the benefits provided by watching foreign films outweighs the minimal effort of reading subtitles. We should not, however, take his statement as implying that creating good subtitles is easy, or that watching a film through subtitles will provide unaltered access to the same meanings as a source-language viewer would have through access to the source-language audio.

The reality is that the prioritisation of naturalisation in translation in the anglophone world can marginalise Asian languages, omitting meanings that would be considered of central importance in the source languages and cultures. Terms, words, and cultural elements that are visible in the original Asian texts are simplified or left out where there is no easily comparator in English. Asian works have often gone through a whitewashing process, with their language becoming anglicised, or westernised, in translation to make the work more palatable for their target audience. One of the most noticeable ways in which this is done is through the naming of characters. While in English, a person will most commonly be referred to by their first name, this is much less normal in East Asian countries, where instead relational terms are used, such as *oppa*. However, in the process of translating into English, this relational nuance is left out as such a term is translated into the character's name. Subtitling does, of course, have particularly exigent constraints in terms of the length of text that can reasonably be shown, and the length of time for which it can be displayed, without having serious impacts on the experience of watching the media at its original speed. Nevertheless, the real height of the barrier between the transmission of core source-language and source-culture meanings to the target-language audience will remain insurmountable unless something is done to change expectations or practice, and measures such as the use of kinship terms, rather than first names (where this reflects the source), is not likely to prevent a viewer from being able to follow the film or series at pace.

5.4 Pragmatic (In)Visibility

More study of the (in)visibility that arises through translation between languages is still needed in the future. The fact that relational dynamics, such as social hierarchy, are encoded much more overtly in Korean and Japanese than in English makes the matter of translating these nuances difficult (as touched upon, a this is an area of difficulty for machines as well as humans). Translators are tasked with the difficulty of how to prioritise acceptability to the target culture against adequacy against the source text. Translators are often criticised for the decisions they have made in translation. Indeed, the increased and increasing linguistic traffic means that there are many more people now in a position to comment in English on translations into that language from their own native languages. Translations of media content are therefore subjected to a kind of enhanced vulnerability, with translators more open to public criticism from those who may feel that certain meanings have not been properly captured. But we *should* look at why translators have made those choices, how they have tried to capture the pragmatic and the cultural meanings of the source while also creating a text that is comprehensible to its target audience, who may have very little knowledge of the source culture and language. Perhaps this post-translation criticism could be interpreted as a form of paratextual commentary. Target-language readers/listeners may be able to enhance their understanding of the source text and source culture by paying attention to this kind of criticism (even if it can be very difficult, as is so often the case with the Internet, to know how much weight to give to a particular source).

Broadly speaking, linguistics in the twenty-first century has focused on human language as embodied in writing and speech. In reality, however, non-verbal communication is also very important to translation as so much meaning is captured in it. In Chapter 4, we observed that in subtitling it is easier to omit the inclusion of any kind of explanatory content for non-verbal signs, as these can easily be considered as outside the scope of translation. However, such omission can be just as detrimental to target-audience understanding as neglecting to translate some of the spoken language. Although it is possible that translators are deliberately relying on target audiences educating themselves on the meaning of physical gestures and the like, whether through regular exposure to such gestures in context through similar media or independent research, further consideration of how best to treat non-verbal language is likely to be worthwhile.

The discussion of (in)visibility arising in translation is sure to be relevant to, and have implications for, translation between language pairs other than English–Japanese or English–Korean. Historically, there has tended to be a huge translational injustice in terms of translation into English from East Asian languages having less prestige in the anglophone world than translations from English have had in much of that region. While so many works have been translated from English into a vast range of Asian languages, Asian works have not had a similar level of representation in English. Although we are a long way from translated literature or media of any kind generally taking a dominant position in the anglophone world, let alone literature or media translated from East Asian languages specifically taking such a position, the success of cultural exports such as *Parasite* and *Squid Game* show how content from this region is becoming more mainstream. It would seem that there is real interest in doing justice to the source content, as reflected in the wide media attention given to criticism of the subtitles for *Squid Game*. There will certainly be some hurdles along the way, but we are optimistic that this growing interest from the public could inspire a new course for translation from other languages into English, with more weight given to reflecting those meanings in the source that have hitherto tended to be ignored.

Bibliography

Akasaka, A. (2016). Kaguya-sama: Love is war. Shueisha.

Ant Studio. (2020–). The Live. Kakao.

Bhabha, H.K. (1994). *The location of culture*. Routledge.

Byon, A.S. (2017). *Modern Korean grammar: A practical guide*. Routledge.

Cho, N.J. (2016). *82 Nyeonsaeng Gim Jiyeong* (82년생 김지영; "Kim Ji-young, Born 1982"). Minumsa.

Cho, S. (2020). Subtitles can't capture the full class critique in "Parasite": Bong Joon-ho's film is even more nuanced and incisive than closed captioning would suggest. GEN, 3 February. https://gen.medium.com/subtitles-cant-capture-the-full-class-critique-in-parasite-27d36748db9d

Cho, Y.-m., Schulz, C., Sohn, H.-M., & Sohn, S.-O. (2019). *Integrated Korean: Beginning 1* (3rd ed.). University of Hawai'i Press.

Clancy, P. (1985). The acquisition of Japanese. In D. Isaac Slobin (Ed.), *The crosslinguistic study of language acquisition: Volume 1: The data* (pp. 373–524). Psychology Press.

Dryden, Y. (2021). From the Preface to Ovid's Epistles. In L. Venuti (Ed.), *The translation studies reader* (pp. 46–50). Routledge. (Original work published 1680).

Elfving-Hwang, J. (2019). K-pop fans are creative, dedicated, and social – we should take them seriously. The Conversation. https://theconversation.com/k-pop-fans-are-creative-dedicated-and-social-we-should-take-them-seriously-119300

Even-Zohar, I. (2005). Polysystem theory revised. In I. Even-Zohar (Ed.), *Papers in culture research* (pp. 38–49). https://citeseerx.ist.psu.edu/viewdoc/download?doi=10.1.1.112.4768&rep=rep1&type=pdf

Even-Zohar, I. (2021). The position of translated literature within the literary polysystem. In L. Venuti (Ed.), *The translation studies reader* (pp. 199–204). Routledge. (Original work published 1978)

Fabbretti, M. (2017). Manga scanlation for an international readership: The role of English as a lingua franca. *Translator* 23(4), 456–73.

Feynman, R. (2022). *Surely you're joking Mr Feynman: Adventures of a curious character*. Vintage Classics. (Original work published 1985)

Gabriel, P. (2014). *Colorless Tsukuru Tazaki and his years of pilgrimage*. Harvill Secker. (Translation of Murakami 2013/2015)

Hasegawa Y. (2012). *The Routledge course in Japanese translation*. Routledge.

Hermans, T. (2020). *Translation in systems: Descriptive and systemic approaches explained*. Routledge.

Higson, A. (2000). The limiting imagination of national cinema. In M. Hjort & S. MacKenzie (Eds.), *Cinema and nation* (pp. 63–74). Routledge.

Hong, E. (2019). *The power of nunchi: The Korean secret to happiness and success.* Penguin Life.

House, J. (2002). Universality versus culture specificity in translation. In A. Riccardi (Ed.), *Translation studies: Perspectives on an emerging discipline* (pp. 92–110). Cambridge University Press.

Ji-Hoon, J. (2019–). The Boxer. LINE Webtoons.

Jin, D. (2016). *New Korean Wave*. University of Illinois Press.

Kang, H. (2007). *Chaesikjuuija* (채식주의자; "The Vegetarian"). Changbi Publishers.

Kiaer, J. (2017). *The Routledge course in Korean translation*. Routledge.

Kiaer, J. (2018). *Translingual words: An East Asian lexical Eecounter with English.* Routledge.

Kiaer, J. (2019). Translating invisibility: The case of Korean–English literary translation. In J. Guest & X.A. Li (Eds.), *Translation and literature in East Asia: Between visibility and invisibility* (pp. 81–117). Routledge.

Kiaer, J. (2020a). *Pragmatic particles: Findings from Asian languages.* Bloomsbury Academic.

Kiaer, J. (2020b). *Study abroad in Korea: Korean language and culture.* Routledge.

Kiaer, J., & Kim, L. (2021a). *Understanding Korean film: A cross-cultural perspective.* Routledge.

Kiaer, J., & Kim, L. (2021b). One-inch-tall barrier of subtitles: Translating invisibility in Parasite. In Y. Kim (Ed.), *Soft power of the Korean wave: Parasite, BTS and drama* (pp. 90–104). Routledge.

Kiaer, J., & Kim, L. (forthcoming). *Embodied words: A guide to the meaning of Asian non-verbal gestures: Through the lens of film.* Routledge.

Kiaer, J., Guest, J., & Li, X.A. (2019). Translation and literature in East Asia: Between visibility and invisibility. Routledge.

Kim, H. (2013). *1999nyeon yeoreum bamsaemyeo haeripoteo beonyeong ijen yeongwonhan naui jarang dwaesseoyo* (1999년 여름 밤새며 해리포터 번역 이젠 영원한 나의 자랑 됐어요; "Translating Harry Potter through the night in 1999 became my life achievement"). Kangwon Domin Ilbo.

Kim, H. (2016). *Harry Potter: Mabeopsaui dol* (해리 포터와 마법사의 돌; "Harry Potter and the Sorcerer's Stone"). Munhaksucheop. (Translation of Rowling 1997/2014)

Kim, L., & Kiaer, J. (2021). Conventions in how Korean films mean. In J. Pflaeging, C. Ng, J. Wildfeuer & J. Bateman (Eds.), *Empirical multimodality research: Methods, evaluations, implications* (pp. 237–58). De Gruyter.

Kitagawa, C., & Lehrer, A. (1990). Impersonal uses of personal pronouns. *Journal of Pragmatics* 14(5), 739–59.

Lee, D. (2015–20). *Yumi's Cells*. LINE Webtoon.

Lee, M. (2002/2007). 호빗 (*Hobbit*). Ssiaseul Ppurineun Saram. (Translation of Tolkien 1937/2011)

Levy, I. (Ed.) (2011). *Translation in modern Japan*. Routledge.

Lyons, J. (1977). *Semantics: Volume I*. Cambridge University Press.

Martin, S.E. (2003). *A reference grammar of Japanese*. Yale University Press. (Original work published 1975)

Matsuoka Y. (2019). ハリー・ポッターと賢者の石 (*Harry Potter to kenja no ishi*). Sayzan-sha Publications. (Translation of Rowling 1997/2014)

Mayer, Y. (2021). *No title*. TikTok. www.tiktok.com/@youngmimayer/video/70138205 57414141189

McClellan, E. (2010). *Kokoro* (translation of original work by Sōseki Natsume). CPI Bookmarque. (Original work published 1968)

Mizuno A. (2012/2013). Stylistic norms in the Early Meiji period: From Chinese influences to European influences. In N. Sato-Rossberg & J. Wakabayashi (Eds.), *Translation and translation studies in the Japanese context* (pp. 92–114). Bloomsbury Academic. (Original work published 2012)

Morris, D. (1979). *Gestures: Their origins and distribution*. Jonathan Cape.

Munday, J. (2001/2016). Introducing *t*ranslation *s*tudies. Routledge.

Murakami, H. (2013/2015). 色彩を持たない多崎つくると、彼の巡⌐の年 (*Colorless Tsukuru Tazaki and his years of pilgrimage*). Bunshun.

Newmark, P. (1981). *Approaches to translation*. Pergamon.

Nida, E. (1964). *Toward a science of translating*. E.J. Brill.

OED (2021). Chaebol, n. OED. www.oed.com/view/Entry/250479?redirectedFrom= chaebol#eid

OED (2022). Tomnoddy, n. OED. www.oed.com/view/Entry/203121?redirectedFrom= tomnoddy#eid

Pasfield-Neofitou, S., & Sell, C. (2016). *Manga vision: Cultural and communicative perspectives*. Monash University Publishing.

Pearce, W.B. (1989). *Communication and the human condition*. Southern Illinois University Press.

Reikai shinkokugo jiten (7th ed.) (2006). Sanseido.

Rosenblatt, K. (2021). Netflix's "Squid Game" is a sensation. Here's why it's so popular. NBC News. www.nbcnews.com/pop-culture/pop-culture-news/netflix-s-squid-game-sensation-here-s-why-it-s-n1280646

Rowling, J.K. (2014). *Harry Potter and the philosopher's stone*. Bloomsbury Publishing. (Original work published 1997)

Sato-Rossberg, N., & Wakabayashi, J. (2012/2013). *Translation and translation studies in the Japanese context*. Bloomsbury Publishing. (Original work published 2012)

Schleiermacher, F. (2021). On the different methods of translating. In L. Venuti (Ed.), *The translation studies reader* (pp. 51–71). Routledge. (Original work published 1813)

Scott, C. (2012). *Translating the perception of text: Literary translation and phenomenology*. Legenda.

Seo, Y., & Owoseje, T. (2022). "Squid Game" star O Yeong-su wins best supporting actor at Golden Globes. CNN Entertainment. https://edition.cnn.com/2022/01/10/entertainment/o-yeong-su-golden-globes-intl-scli/index.html

Seta, T. (2016). ホビットの冒険 (*Hobbit no bōken*). Iwanami Shoten. (Original work published 1979; translation of Tolkien 1937/2011)

Shibatani, M. (2005). *The languages of Japan*. Cambridge University Press. (Original work published 1990)

Sohn, H.-M. (2006). *Korean language in culture and society*. University of Hawai'i Press.

Song, J.J. (2005). *The Korean language: Structure, use and context*. Routledge.

Soonkki. (2010). Cheese in Trap. Naver.

Steiner, G. (1998). *After Babel: Aspects of language and translation* (3rd ed.). Oxford University Press. (Original work published 1975)

Suzuki, T. (1976). Language and behaviour in Japan: The conceptualization of personal relations. *Japan Quarterly* 23, 255–66.

Tanaka, L. (2016). Impolite language in manga. In S. Pasfield-Neofitou & C. Sell, *Manga Vision: Cultural and communicative perspectives* (pp. 209–26). Monash University Publishing.

Tolkien, J.R.R. (2011). *The hobbit, or there and back again*. HarperCollins Publishers. (Original work published 1937)

Toury, G. (2012). *Descriptive translation studies – and beyond* (2nd ed.). John Benjamins. (Original work published 1995)

Venuti, L. (2017). *The translator's invisibility: A history of translation*. Routledge. (Original work published 1995)

Venuti, L. (2019). *Contra instrumentalism: A translation polemic*. University of Nebraska Press.

Willemen, P. (2006). The nation revisited. In Valentina Vitali & Paul Willemen (Eds.), *Theorising national cinema* (pp. 29–43). BFI and Palgrave Macmillan.

Yamamoto, S. (2014). ホビットゆきてかえりし物語 [*Hobbit yukitekaerishi monogatari*]. Harashobo. (Original work published 2012; translation of Tolkien 1937/2011)

Yanabu, A. (2004). *Hon'yakugo seiritsu jijō*. Iwanami Shinsho. (Original work published 1982)

Yonezawa, Y. (2021). *The mysterious address term* anata *"you" in Japanese*. John Benjamins Publishing Company.

Yoon, S.-S. (2015). Korean honorifics beyond politeness markers: Change of footing through shifting of speech style. In M. Terkourafi (Ed.), *Interdisciplinary perspectives on im/politeness* (pp. 97–120). John Benjamins Publishing Company.

Filmography

Aoki, Y. (2004–6). *Yakitate!! Japan* (焼き立て！！ジャぱん; "Freshly Baked!! Japan"). Sunrise.

Bong, J. (2019). *Parasite*. CJ Entertainment.

Hwang, D. (2021). *Ojingeo Geim* (오징어 게임; "Squid Game"). Netflix.

Im, S. (2010). *Hanyeo* (해녀; "The Housemaid"). Sidus FNH.

Ishihara, T. (2011). *Nichijou* (日常; "Everyday"). Kyoto Animation.

Jang, H. (2017). *Taeksi Unjeonsa* (택시운전사; "A Taxi Driver"). Showbox.

Kim, D. (2019). *82 Nyeonsaeng Gim Jiyeong* (82년생 김지영; "Kim Ji-young Born: 1982"). Lotte Cultureworks.

Lee, J. (2015). *Sado* (사도; "The Throne"). Showbox.

Yamazaki, M. (2020). *Sleepy Princess in the Demon Castle* (魔王城でおやすみ; "Good Night in Demon Castle"). Doga Kobo.

Index

Note: Page numbers in **bold** indicate tables and page numbers in *italics* indicate figures.

Printed in the USA
CPSIA information can be obtained
at www.ICGtesting.com
LVHW022040271223
767550LV00005B/706